SPIRITUAL HUMANISM

SPIRITUAL HUMANISM

Louis Carini

Copyright © 2000 by Louis Carini.

Library of Congress Number: 00-192106

ISBN: Softcover 0-7388-3708-3

All rights reserved. No part of this book may be reproduced or transmitted in any form or by any means, electronic or mechanical, including photocopying, recording, or by any information storage and retrieval system, without permission in writing from the copyright owner.

This book was printed in the United States of America.

To order additional copies of this book, contact:
Xlibris Corporation
1-888-7-XLIBRIS
www.Xlibris.com
Orders@Xlibris.com

CONTENTS

Introduction: Spiritual and Rational Humanisms   9

Chapter I
Consciousness and Disinterested Interest   16

Chapter II
God, and The Big Bang   25

Chapter III
The Evolution of Consciousness   36

Chapter IV
Physics and the Science of
Anthropomorphic Optics   50

Chapter V
Thinking, Artificial Intelligence,
and Why People Act as They Do   66

Chapter VI
Psychologizing Physics   81

Chapter VII
Rewriting Human History   95

Chapter VIII
Spiritual Humanism   109

Chapter IX
Self Determinations   118

Chapter X
    Fostering Disinterested Interest   128

Conclusions   140

INTRODUCTION: SPIRITUAL AND RATIONAL HUMANISMS

Even ancient definitions of humanity suggested that we are the rational animals. Rationality, however, looking at our own times and earlier ones, appears to be a quality that is only sometimes achieved. Ernst Cassirer in *Essay on Man* redefined the human animal more broadly. He wrote, "instead of defining man as an *animal rationale* we should define him as an *animal symbolicum*." Defining us as symbolic animals allows for irrationality as well as rationality to be the outcome. Though we certainly do not appear to be the only animals who use symbols, it does, indeed, seem to be the case that humanity displays an inveterate commitment to them.

We speak a symbolic language, we read and write in symbols, we dream in symbols when we are asleep, and we flesh out our other dreams in symbolic forms in art, religion, history, and even in science. I include science in our symbolic dreams, not only because of what scientists tell us about how their discoveries may come to them, but because otherwise we may forget that scientific theories are woven out of *imagination*, a *symbolic* realm, and end in the *symbols* of abstract formulae. It is true, however, that these scientific formulae, expressed in symbolic forms allow the scientists' to predict actual physical events, so I can understand some objection to my calling them dreamers. However, some years ago a very good book by Arthur Koestler about the historical development of physical science and astronomy was entitled *The Sleepwalkers,* and for very good reasons.

It is not only symbols that I am emphazing in the definition of humanity. I want in this book to call particular attention to the spiritual as a dimension of our humanity; it is, by my lights, an essential dimension, and one that is peculiarly ours. I do this, knowing that the term *spiritual* will jar some of those who espouse rationality to the exclusion of any other emphasis in humanity. Yet, I also notice that some humanists at least, are beginning to have qualms about an over commitment to rationality. I know that I do.

I think that the problem for some humanists has been that art, unlike most of science, is not necessarily rational—though both are symbolic. But though art may not be rational altogether, it is not necessarily irrational either. In this instance we do have a neutral term: arational. Given the extremes that the two dichotomous terms anchor, it might be preferable to opt for the neutral term. But art is such a lively, and even vibrant human activity, that it deserves a more positive treatment. After all art has a long and illustrious history. Spanning more than thirty millenia, as we now know that it does, art deserves to be treated in its own terms.

Art is most of all expressive. Art works indicate an expressive valuation of our world and a valuing of what is expressive. Art involves our capacity to be wholly involved in something just for how and what it is—not for its *usefulness*. Many years ago now, Ernst Schachtel in his sadly neglected book *Metamorphosis* wrote:

> Human perception is not only in the service of the question . . . "How can I use you . . . ? [but] "Who or what are you who are part of this same world of which I am a part?"

He continued:

> A painter who is able to be completely absorbed, again and again often for many hours and days in an object that arouses his interest will be the one who enlarges his and sometimes man's scope of perception and experience. A painter may spend many days, weeks or months, or even years, in looking at some mountain as Cezanne did . . . without ever tiring of it and without ceasing to find something new in it.

Schachtel chose the artist to illustrate the peculiarly human stance of openness to expression. But the artist, or anyone able to be drawn into something *for its own sake* rather than for some practical purpose for or use by us, indicates to me a spiritual dimension to our humanity. There was no practical use for the paintings Cezanne created, for he was fifty-six before he had his first one-man show. There was also no practical use for Einstein's theory of relativity when he published it. It was accepted at once by physicists—for aesthetic reasons, and for its own sake. I call this special attitude displayed by Cezanne and Einstein one of *disinterested interest*. When we take a deep interest in anything for its own sake we display at the same time a state personally of *dis*interest, but one of great interest in the phenomenon. This special attitude arises out of our human consciousness. It is consciousness which releases us from our direct relation to objects and persons. It is also that same consciousness from whence derives the spiritual side of human nature.

At the same time I believe that spirituality *per se* is not the answer. For it is not that other worldly spirituality that I aim to foster here, but that spiritual dimension that is already existent in humanity's consciousness. *Our* humanism is infused with that expressive and valuing spirit which arises especially in our consciousness. The word "spirituality," for me at least, carries with it too much of the quality of a commitment to another life beyond the one we live within daily. The *Compact Edition of the Oxford English Dictionary* defines spirituality as: "the condition of being spiritual . . ." and "as opposed to . . . worldly interests." I do not see the spiritual humanist condition as *being* spiritual, as the word "spirituality" implies, but as involving a spiritual side that is fully human. Spiritual humanism not only does not preclude worldly interests, but fosters them. It fosters them, however, in the light of the *spiritedness* arising from our consciousness. Those worldly interests whether we want them to do so or not, simply do include a spiritual aspect. A spiritual humanism is about human beings in their worldly worlds, not in some celestial sphere beyond this life. But we are always in our worldly worlds as beings who have our consciousness at the center of our lives. At the same time a spiritual humanism does not preclude a strictly religious commitment. There are multitudes of persons full of human caring who hold Deistic beliefs. Religious persons can and do have humanistic bents. But humanism as a commitment locates its central concerns with humanity rather than with a Deity or with organized religious beliefs and commitments. Or at least that is the spiritual humanism that I propose in this little book.

I see art, especially artistry, as central to the enterprise of spiritual humanism. Some thirty thousand years ago artists were at work in what is now France. Their works have often been interpreted in practical terms—as having some useful purpose, of expressing their hopes for a successful hunt by this investment in the drawings of the animals. But the most recent find casts a shadow on this interpretation. The newly discovered ancient paintings include animals that were not hunted, and the artistry in these, as well as the ones at Lascaux, suggest an artistry carried out *for its own sake.* That which is done for its own sake is an example of *disinterested interest.* A disinterested interest is peculiarly human. The established notion that the works of those ancient artists served only a practical function insults their art and artistry. And it especially insults the human spirit that underlies all artistry engaged in *for its own sake.*

I wish to explore a different set of ideas that are more generous to those artists, and is more inclusive of their art and artistry. I assume that from the actual evidence they provide, from the ubiquitous religious yearnings of humanity itself, and from the evidence that people have always cared for and cherished their children, that there is and has always been a spiritual dimension to humanity. The generations of humanity would not even currently exist had human beings always and only 'lived for bread alone.'

This evidence of a spiritual quality in us human beings lies especially in the fact of human consciousness. I see a man raise his arm in the distance. That is what I am aware of. I ask myself, 'Is he waving at me?' This everyday example immediately shows a consciousness beyond mere awareness. With that simple question I have reflected upon what was in my awareness. Such a reflection upon an awareness, upon any awareness, I call consciousness. I call a reflective awareness consciousness, because it is an awareness carried to a second level. Then, perhaps, I turn around to see whether there is someone behind me at whom he is waving. Finding that there is no one, I look back and see that the man has lowered his arm and is walking away. Then I think to myself, 'He was just stretching his arm.' This last comment is an example of what I call consciousness, because I was reflecting upon the fact of my awareness of an awareness. If I reflect upon this tendency in all of us to be able to reflect upon such occurences, I would be reflecting upon consciousness itself. There can be, of course, that painful self-consciousness of adolescence. But there is also a non self referential and positive side to our reflective consciousnesses. One can consider, as I have been doing, just how to define consciousness itself, and reflect upon its nature so as to be able to outline its qualities in and of itself. In doing this I came to the conclusion that consciousness is best defined as the awareness of any awareness of any thing or event. Awareness of any awareness includes, of course, the self, but is not restricted, as the phrase has been, to the self. So it is then that a reflection on awarenesses and upon consciousness apart from oneself, and without self reference can also occur. A reflective consciousness is probably a quality of which only human beings are possessed.

It is this same consciousness that is evidenced in every adult human being which gives us a sense of a conscience—of a voice within which tells what to do or what not to do. It can even give us a sense of another being resident within us with whom we have discussions. It is, I believe, the source of those who experience angels within them or about them. But that is my opinion, and I could be wrong. Consciousness is especially the human realm within which the sense of what I am calling spirit arises. Consciousness is also the ability within us which gives rise to an aesthetic sense and to rationality too. Rationality arises out of a reflective process that can take place only in consciousness. Our schools and colleges have a great commitment to fostering rationality. I believe that they largely fail to foster either an aesthetic attitude, or, and especially, one attuned to human *values*. That is why I have been focussing on an aesthetic attitude rather than rationality here. I believe that we need to foster aesthetic attitudes, and an educated sense of values to at least the same extent that we have fostered thinking and rationality.

Some years ago I had gone to the Chicago Art Institute, and on the first day I was there I had come across a painting of Cezanne's—a still life of a vase with flowers—that I had only seen in reproduction. I had thought it to be one of his worst paintings. Now I saw how wrong I had been. I found it to be a truly fine painting, and in my mind I apologized to Cezanne. With consciousness that was easy for me to do, and I think it is a quality that one way or another we have all experienced and do also do. I was admiring the masterful way he had related the colors and forms to one another to achieve his fine composition when I was interrupted by a man of whom I had been vaguely aware. He said, "Isn't it true that a painting like that might be worth a million dollars?" I said, "Oh, yes, perhaps millions." And he turned to his wife whom I realized he had been haranging all along and said, "See, I told you so." And off he went talking away.

I cite this example, because it illustrates that it is possible with consciousness to take attitudes. I was able to take what I call an aesthetic attitude—which meant that I was paying attention to the relations of colors and forms within the painting for their own sake—not for any reasons extraneous to those. I wasn't wondering what the vase was made of, or what kinds of flowers those were. And I was not, as my vociferous momentary companion was, assessing the painting's monetary worth, its market value—though I was able to change my attitude to do that to answer him. These latter two are *not* aesthetic attitudes. They are practical in their concerns; the aesthetic attitude is not practical. The aesthetic attitude has no practical use; its function is exhausted in what it is, and in what it brings simply in terms of itself.

Without art to guide us we would not be able as easily to take this amazingly human attitude of a personally *disinterested, but deep interest in events outside outselves*. It is the quality of a spiritual side existent in consciousness, and in our reflective consciousness, that gives us this quality that is so central to a spiritual humanism.

Disinterested interest is a function of human consciousness. Both of them indicate a spiritual quality resident within us. Rationality, too, is a function of disinterested interest. That, I believe, is why we have prized rationality for these many centuries. But it is rationality *and* an aesthetic attitude together which are desparately needed for humanity to take full advantage of what human consciousness offers us.

In this book I am in part giving witness to my own quest to bring together the rational and the aesthetic. The spiritual nature of our human consciousness gives rise to both. I believe that through this definition of consciousness we can also bring our spiritual lives into a true raprochement with the values we express in our lives. In the process I certainly have no intention of constraining anyone to a view of the human spirit that requires the espousal of a particular set of spiritual or religious views. I aim at freeing all of our views from the constraits of dogma. My aim is to give each person the right to espouse his or her individual sense of the outcome of the spiritual in each one, whether it be a part of an organized religion or a completely idiosyncratic personal expression. But I also intend to insist that there is a spiritual side to all human beings that for far too long has been overlooked. It resides in the fact of human awareness and consciousness whose components I try to expose in this book. And I intend to try to show that the ramifications of that spiritual quality hold deep and important consequences for human beings.

CHAPTER I

Consciousness and Disinterested Interest

The blind and deaf Helen Keller lived from the age of nineteen months until she was six years and about nine months without language—yet she had a kind of consciousness. She communicated, of course. Even the lowest animals communicate. She was able to communicate her desires and demands through ingenious gestures. She describes how she communicated with her older, sighted black companion when she wished to hunt for bird's eggs in the grass by leaning to touch the ground and making a fist for an egg. She always determined, with insistent gestures, that it would be she who would carry the eggs home, because the other might fall and break them. That incident required that she be aware of the fact that one of them might fall and break the eggs, and also be aware that she was the one to be trusted with the task. She displayed an awareness of another awareness—consciousness, according to my definition. She showed no awareness, of course, that the sighted are less likely to fall and break the eggs. She was unaware then, apparently, that the sighted could see. She learned that when she had acquired language.

Our son, Peter, at two and one-half years was introduced for the first time to eating cherries. He hit a stone with his first bite and looked at me somewhat aggreivedly. I hastened, rather guiltily, to tell him that we did not eat the stones, but if he were to swallow one it would do no harm. I showed him how to bite so that the stone was to one side of our teeth so that we missed hitting the stone, and it could then be removed. He went on to eat them in what seemed to me to be a thoughtful manner. After a while he said, "Birds eat seeds, but I don't." I thought, "Consciousness." He was not only aware, but he was aware of his own state of awareness. His was, as Helen Keller's was also, a reflective awareness. Though Helen was at an older age than Peter was when she displayed her consciousness, the situations seem to be similar in their complexity. Language and development with age both usually have their effects upon consciousness.

When Anne Sullivan began teaching the manual alphabet to Helen Keller in early March of 1887, Helen was six years and eight months. Her age was one of several important and fortuitous factors that came together a month later to give Helen language, and a consequent boost to her consciousness. The Swiss epistemologist, Jean Piaget, determined that the ages from six to eight are central in allowing the child to be aware of more than one aspect of a test situation at the same time. That is, when it does not arise out of the child's personal interest as occurred with Peter and Helen Keller. Before the age of six to eight the child is likely to note only one dimension, so, for example, pouring the same water from a short and wide beaker into a taller and narrower one leads the child to conclude that the *amount* has increased. After age seven children usually grasp that the amount of water has remained the same. An important distinction exists between the two examples earlier and this finding, for here the awareness of a second awareness arises in a test situation that also is one that occurs apart from the child's *personally interested* interest. The situation does not involve any personal need, and yet there is an integration of awarenesses that allows for the successful solution. Though the child's interest in the task is probably not entirely *dis*interested, the task differs from one that arises out of the child's own direct interest. It is the two events out there that are at issue, and not something related to the child's egocentric interests, as were my son's and as Helen's were about the eggs. I stress this because Helen Keller remained egocentrically tied to her own *self* interests until she acquired language.

Anne Sullivan reports on the month long series of tussles she had trying to domesticate the wild and egocentered Helen Keller. She reports one such altercation that occurred just one week before the famous incident at the well, and immediately after obtaining the Keller's agreement to allow her to discipline Helen when necessary:

> Only a few hours after my talk with Captain and Mrs. Keller (and they had agreed to everything), Helen took a notion that she wouldn't use her napkin at table. I think she wanted to see what would happen. I attempted several times to put the napkin round her neck; but each time she tore it off and threw it on the floor and finally began to kick the table. I took her plate away and started to take her out of the room. Her father objected...

But apparently such outbursts had become less frequent, though Helen remained very much centered on her appetites and her egocentered desires. She suffered caresses from no one except her mother, and offered affection to no one—not even her mother. When Anne Sullivan brought up the napkin incident the next day, she reports the following outcome when she demonstrated to Helen through gestures the wrongness of her behavior the previous evening at dinner: "I think she understood perfectly well; for she slapped her hand two or three times and shook her head." Anne Sullivan 's training was having an effect: Helen was aware of her naughty behavior and her responsibility in it. But she had no words to convey that, so *she slapped her own hand* as a replacement for the words that we so easily think to ourselves.

What language brings to human consciousness becomes plain if we look at Helen's relations before the famous incident at the well and what happened immediately after that. As I said, Helen Keller expressed no affection for anyone. Though Helen now slept with Anne Sullivan and was as dependent upon her as Sullivan could make the situation, Helen kept her distance. She continued to allow no caresses and never offered any herself. On the morning of that fateful incident at the well Anne Sullivan had been trying to teach Helen that her old rag doll could be called doll, just as the new doll she had given Helen on her arrival was so named. I say *named*, because Helen, unlike the rest of us did not know the difference between names and words. She thought that all the words she had been taught were really the proper names for things. She thought that the doll was actually named "Doll." She thought the dog was named "Dog." She had not grasped the conceptual nature of words. *Concepts* stand for, represent, and relate many items to one another. Names name one person. The term "ocean" relates the cold and much smaller Arctic to the much larger and warmer Pacific Ocean and, despite their great differences makes them both the *same*. The concepts that our words represent integrate and relate events and facts that differ in many significant ways. But we ignore the differences once we have acquired the concept.

Names, on the other hand, name one person or animal: Anne or Rover, for example. Helen had acquired by March 31 what Anne Sullivan thought were twenty-one words, but they were to Helen twenty-one names. Here they are as Anne Sullivan wrote them out:

> Those with a cross after them are words she had asked for herself: *Doll, mug, pin, key, dog, hat, cup, box, water, milk,* candy, eye (x), finger (x), toe (x), head (x), cake, baby, mother, sit, stand, walk.

The terms that she had asked for were all parts of her own body. She had not asked for the others, but had been taught them by Anne Sullivan. (Note that *water* was one of them.) I believe that Helen's own interests were egocentric in that they were all oriented around her body and the direct satisfaction of her needs. The reward of cake stood high in her orientation toward the world.

On the fateful morning she asked for the name of the first item that was not a part of her body. It was *water*. Perhaps she was sitting in it? Water, pronounced by her as "Wah-wah" was the only sound she retained from before her illness. (Anne Sullivan was apparently unaware of this fact.) I presume she said it many times to quench her fevered thirst during her terrible illness. But the bath water does not seem to her to have been related by her to "Wah-wah." After all, bath water is warm, soapy, and is not used to quench one's thirst. Perhaps bath water and drinking water were not in Helen's awarenesses as one and the same item. Helen's awarenesses from the remote past were not easily available to her. It must have taken some effort on her part, and a strong personal interest to communicate to her companion about the egg hunting. And I believe that her awarenesses were especially hard to integrate over time, for Helen had little sense of time before the well-incident. Her aunt tells of Helen's wanting to arise and have breakfast at midnight. The aunt indulged her in this. Time, unlike space, is not apprehended merely through the senses. We humans can only *conceive of time*. We do not perceive time directly. We perceive now, and again now, but to integrate the two there has to be a removal from the sense experience into the nonsensory experience of concepts. Then we can know that time has passed, for our *thought,* in consciousness, now tells us that this is another time. Helen Keller's conception of time was vague, because it was hindered by her lack of worded concepts.

After breakfast Anne Sullivan remembered having just taught Helen the word for water—forgetting that she had listed it as having been learned earlier—and took Helen to the well to try to break into the confusion Helen displayed of identifying what was in the mug with the act of drinking. Anne Sullivan reports:

> This morning, while she was washing, she wanted to know the name for "water." When she wants to know the name of anything, she points to it and pats my hand. I spelled "w-a-t-e-r" and thought no more about it until after breakfast. . . . We went out to the pump-house, and I made Helen hold her mug under the spout while I pumped. As the cold water gushed forth, filling the mug, I spelled "w-a-t-e-r" in Helen's free hand. The word coming so close upon the sensation of cold water rushing over her hand seemed to startle her. She dropped

the mug and stood as one transfixed. A new light came into her face. She spelled "w-a-t-e-r" several times. Then she dropped to the ground and asked for its name....

In that instant Helen Keller regained her long since lost art of using words as *concepts* as well as as names.

Helen Keller could once again think in concepts instead of in direct perceptual awarenesses. Of course, she could think and had been thinking—really very well all along. But she had not been thinking with the advantage that worded concepts, as thoughts apart from the present sensory awareness, gives to all the rest of us. Thinking in thoughts instead of in direct sense experiences gives us the freedom to think easily about what is not present. And we all do this just naturally because we see, and in seeing we clearly demarcate one object off from other objects, and place them as near or far. Vision gives us our three dimensional clarity and clear demarcation of one thing from another as touch does not as well. And then we hear those clearly perceived objects referred to in sounds, and we come to grasp quite directly the relations between visual image, sound image, and meaning. Thus it is that we come to use words conceptually from about the age of twenty-one months on the average. The nineteen month-old, young Helen Keller had had that ability and, I believe, lost it with the illness that robbed her of sight and hearing.

Now she had the linguistic concepts back again with the word spelled into her hand. In this case it was the overdetermined *water*. Grasping now that the word stood for any, and every water, warm or cold, soapy or drinkable, she suddenly longed for words. That was why she fell to the ground and asked for its name. Helen Keller must have been over and over confronted by the question: *What is this that is constantly pressing me at the bottoms of my feet whether I walk or run?* The ground could now reside in her head and not over and over again as constant awarenesses at the bottoms of her feet whenever she walked or ran, of fell down upon it in fury. Without our word based concepts Helen Keller's consciousness also lacked the *spiritual* dimension that our clarified consciousness gives us. Consciousness is of what is not present as well as of what is present. Though consciousness has its more ephemeral seeming, but natural beginnings in the more complex fashion that Piaget proved at the average age of seven, Helen Keller entered it at the age of six years and nine months. The Roman Catholic Church knew this centuries ago, for it was at that age that one is taught to go to confession to confess one's sins. It is the beginning of conscience's eerie voice within us, that phantom voice that lets us know that what we are about to do is wrong—or after doing it, was wrong.

All of these multilayered factors that been held in abeyance by the blindness and deafness, and the lack of conceptualized words especially, struck Helen Keller at that one instant at the well. It changed her forever. It changed her mode of learning: She doubled her vocabulary that afternoon. It changed her mode of thought: She began to think in words, not names. And more important, she began to think of another person as a separate person. She asked for Anne Sullivan's name. This heretofore egocentered child asked for the name of another being. Continual self reference became immediately a mode of the past. Indeed, in time Helen Keller became a model of *disinterested* interest, even about all of her own doings and accomplishments.

But even more important than the change in thought brought on by her new consciousness was her change in feeling. Anne Sullivan wrote:

> Helen got up this morning like a radiant fairy. She has flitted from object to object, asking the name of everything and kissing me for very gladness. Last night when I got in bed, she stole into my arms of her own accord and kissed me for the first time, and I thought my heart would burst, so full was it of joy.

I say that the change in feeling was even more important than the change in thought, because it was the change in feeling that brought about the great change in Helen's values. From caring only about her own wishes and desires, caring only about cake and other sweets, Helen Keller moved to caring about another human being: Anne Sullivan.

A deeply involved but personally *distinterested interest,* one that we all understand had commenced for Helen Keller.

The change in feeling had many far reaching effects upon her actions. She had known her sister, Mildred, only as Baby until the time of the well. Once when she had found Mildred asleep in *her* doll's bed she had overturned the bed and the child would have been hurt, had her mother not caught her in time. Helen had no qualms then about that incident. But now she was able to learn that Mildred and she shared the same mother and father. They were *related.* Indeed, they were closely related. Mildred, now grasped as her sister, her close relative, became one of her most beloved persons. Mildred took on *meaning.* For as John Dewey said, meaning inheres in relations. What is unrelated to us is meaningless, but what is related to us is meaningful. Mildred began to mean what that person would mean to Helen for the rest of her life: her beloved only sister. The consciousness that arose with thought consists of relational terms for thought, but it also consists of relational terms for the values which we understand through how they feel to us.

Consciousness is not only concerned with our thoughts, it is also concerned with the feelings that tell us the values of things and of the events in our lives. Helen Keller's consciousness led to the thoughts that can lead to rationality, but consciousness also led to the feelings that deepened her sense of values. The same is true for all of us human beings who have consciousness. And that includes all of us. The spirit that shows itself in consciousness transforms both thought and feeling. Once a reflective consciousness is present, all adult human beings can reflect not only on the ideas they encounter, but also on their values—what matters to them, what they care about most deeply, perhaps what they need for self respect. Consciousness as the basis of reflective thought affects the nature of our thought, and that same reflective thought also affects the nature of the values by which we live. Disinterested interest in our surroundings can become one of our felt values. Rationality can become one of its value outcomes and an aesthetic attitude can become another.

Consciousness does not remain at the seven year-old's level.

Puberty brings with it an increase in the ability to think in more abstract terms and with a heightened imagination. More changes lead to a more increasingly complex consciousness throughout adolescence and early adulthood. And I know from experience that a deepened consciousness can develop even during the early forties. Research on all of these changes is, of course, lacking. But this brief introduction to the complex nature of human consciousness as the basis for disinterested interest can serve as sufficient basis for considering the issues it brings to the fore in the remainder of the book.

CHAPTER II

God, and The Big Bang

Cardinal Nicholas of Cusa was not burned at the stake even though, according to Ernst Cassirer in *The Individual and the Cosmos in Renaissance Philosophy*, he wrote: "There is no form of faith so low, so abominable. . . . polytheism is not excluded. For wherever *gods* are honoured . . . the idea of the divine must be presupposed." He was not burned at the stake, because the Roman Catholic church had not yet been touched by the rise of Protestentism. He wrote in the 1440s, and for writing words no more heretical than those, Giordano Bruno was in 1600 burned at the stake. We no longer need to fear the inquisition and the stake, but I fear that our thought has not attained the flexibility displayed by Cusa. If we can prevail upon ourselves to achieve the openness that he showed then, we may reach new levels of religious thought not now available to us. The result might well be the outcome that he envisaged: "the sword, hate, envy, and all evil shall disappear, and all shall know that in the multiplicity of rites, there is only one religion." That one religion apparently would be the one of whatever or Whoever first set everything off in the beginning, if there was one, with that well-known big bang, or was it the Big Bang?!—if there truly was a big bang. I say that last because there is a *theory* set forth by physical scientists that there was a big bang. I suppose that if it were a Whoever rather than a whatever, that set the universe off, then that could then in a sense give us a clue to God's religion. But Cusa's conclusion is that we cannot know, indeed, on logical grounds, we can never know what religion God would epouse. That is the issue of this chapter, that and some of the consequences that follow from it.

Nicholas Cusanus was not only a cardinal of the Roman Catholic Church, but he was also a true scholar and mathematician, and it was his utilization of mathematical ideas as applied to religious issues that led to his radical conclusions. The view that the Roman Catholic Church had derived from Aristotelean ideas resulted in a graduated universe and a graduated heavenly one. The universe was ordered from lower to higher, the earth at the lowest level, water and air next, and fire as the most remote from the earth. Fire strove toward the heavens where the fiery heavenly bodies formed perfect circular motions. This theory reigned for nearly two millenia. The Church based its hierarchy on a similarly graduated scheme. Just as the earth had its lower and higher, the formless earth to the perfectly formed celestial spheres in their perfect circular movements, so too do the heavens, the religious heavens have their hierarchy. The finiteness of the earthbound events and the infiniteness of the Deity were conceived of as upon a continuum. The finite gradually drifted into the infinite. It was this conception of a continuum from the finite to the infinite in a graded fashion that the mathematician in Cusanus could not accept.

One sense of infiniteness is the one that arises from the number series as 1, 2, 3, etc. ad infinitum. It seems to me that that sense of infinity does seem to place it on a continuum with the finite series of $n + 1$. That is, even though it goes on into infinity, the numbers apparently still do go on into infinity in increments of one. But this does not appear to be Cusanus way of thinking about infinity. A problem with that view of infinity arose for him because, as he said, the finite and the infinite have no common denominator, no measures that the two share in common, so that the means of measurement in the one cannot be certain to fit the means of measuring in the other. "Finiti et infinite nulla proportio." According to my feeble recollection of Latin this means, roughly speaking, that the finite and the infinite are incomparable; they lack a common denominator that would give each of them the same means of measurement. The increments of $n + 1$ while providing an infinite series do, indeed, retain the same incremental scale throughout. His conclusion appears to be that in an infinite series the exact, same scale does not, or at least, *may not* adhere to the n + 1 in our finite series. We do not know whether at some point in the infinite, a new scale might arise, and he concluded: We cannot know.

We can measure finite events in feet, kilometers, miles, or even light years. But we have no comparable measures that fit an infinite space—none of the above apply. And now, as I understand it, we do not know whether our universe itself is finite or infinite, though the idea that it is infinite has been taking over. Cusanus' point is that to measure infinite space we would have to have some means of measurement appropriate for infinite space. The fact is that we have no such means, and we have no idea of what such a means would be. And, in fact, we cannot even have any hope that someday such a means could become available to us. It cannot happen, and it will not. Thus, it will no longer do, *logically*, to place our finite measures, as large as they may be, along side infinite—but unknown and unknowable—ones, and assume that they are upon a continuum. The break is really a gulf, and an absolute one. It is no longer possible to maintain the notion that there is a relative break between the finite and the infinite. The chasm in Cusa's terms is unbridgable. The older view of the infinite he believed was mistaken, because it failed to grasp that no measure, not even our modern light years can come any closer than an inch to measures appropriate for infinity. We do not know, we cannot know the measures appropriate for measuring within infinite nonboundaries. The finite and the infinite are absolutely incomparable. Therefore not only is it the case that we do not know any such measures, but on logical grounds such measures are always precluded from us. We cannot know them.

It appears to me that Cusanus conceived of the finite and the infinite as if they were two separate realms, each having its own qualities in such a sharply defined fashion that the two could never become part of one realm. Then he went on to apply this conception of the finite and the infinite to humanity and to God. God, he assumed was infinite. And we, of course, are clearly finite. So according to his assumptions, we cannot know God. Indeed, we are enjoined by logic, when we accept his assumptions, to conclude that no human being could ever grasp the nature of the Deity. Therefore, according to the demands of logic, his views with which I began this chapter, actually would have to follow from his premises: All faiths are equally *wrong*. It is not the case that we cannot know whether this one or that one is the right one, but on the logic following from his assumptions, all must of necessity, all, must be wrong! No one can know the infinite God's religious choice. The orthodox view had been that in assuming that this one or that one was His true religion, we might be wrong, but now the orthordox view must be that any and every religion espoused by us human and necessarily finite beings, must of necessity be wrong. Just as there is no unit of comparison between the finite and the infinite realms, there is no means by which we could even guess the nature of an infinite God or what religion God might espouse from our necessarily finite perspective. Earlier I had thought that Cusanus' position gave us one chance in an infinity of chances that we might know the Deity; but I have had to recognize that never knowing the Deity has now become what I, and all of us, according to Cusa's logic, must accept as so.

Please understand, his conceptions arise from *assumptions* that we can either make or refuse to make. If we prefer to reject his assumptions, then none of what I am offering here need give us a moment's pause. If, however, we wish to entertain his assumptions, then I do believe that much that is thought provoking would follow. It is the consequences that follow from even a provisional acceptance of his assumptions that I wish to examine here. They are thought provoking, indeed. And perhaps as Cusa said, then: "the sword, hate, envy . . . shall disappear, and all shall know . . . there is only one religion."

Current doctrine has the universe expanding from a big bang. The contraction of something—current doctrine has it in totally *physical* terms, but that is only because nothing of the spirit fits current physical doctrine or measurement—was so great that we, and all we can, or will be able to survey with the now repaired space telescope, is the result of its continuing expansion. This big bang according to current doctrine is not conscious, and accordingly, I suggest could not achieve our states of consciousness, because it is according to current *doctrine* physical only. No one appears to presume that it consists of our type of thalamo-cortical system which gives us our consciousness. But its force, and the continuing force the big bang let loose, goes on—apparently without consciousness—working within and changing the universe. Recall that I differentiate awarenesses from consciousness. Consciousness consists in our awareness of awarenesses. I suggest that the big bang force as it is currently conceived could not have our consciousness. Not even the consciousness of a three year old child. This big bang force, I suggest, is in great trouble; it clearly needs us to provide it with consciousness, or at least the means to delineate how our consciousness could have arisen. According to current doctrine there is no consciousness associated with the big bang. We, however, *are* endowed with consciousness, after all. I have been here separating the physical big bang, and the force it let loose, sharply from God, though I am aware that many people simply believe in both, but separately, and others only in one. I, however, see no harm in temporarily conceiving of identifying the two in a new conception for the purposes of our discussion.

One of the greatest effects in the past has been to give this newly conceived Big Bang Force—when it was not a big bang force, but was God who created the earth—some human-like qualities. Some people suggest that God punishes wrong doers in an after life; some don't. But does my new Big Bang Force subscribe to our categories at all? Whatever we answer, it would have to be based upon an assumption, because we do not know—and utilizing Nicholas of Cusa's *assumptions*—we cannot know whether either God, or in the new formulation of my new Big Bang Force, even subscribe to any of our finite, human categories. Both of the older positions, the big bang and conventional religions, seem to agree that the evolution of the universe and the earth and its inhabitants arise from one or the other of these sources. Once again we have a split, for one group sees our evolution as purely a physical one, but with a consciousness somehow arising from the physical, and the other is predisposed toward a spiritual force they call God from whom human souls and the material world both arise. But, following my assumptions, we do not know whether these assumptions about physical and spiritual categories are actually held by either God or this new Big Bang Force. They are both finite, human conceptions—the new Big Bang Force, so far as I know, mine alone. Such finite conceptions of any kind cannot be held by the strict big bang proponents, for physical events are by definition without awareness or consciousness. I say *conceptions* because I *believe* that all of these notions arose in humanity. And whether inspired or otherwise, conceiving of anything is on the basis of our thought and feeling. But the new Big Bang Force, unless it has our consciousness, is not likely to conceive of matters in a fashion such as we do. God, however, being conceived in our image, or we in His as some hold, might well be considered to have consciousness—indeed, omniscience, some assume. There are, then, consequences dependent upon which assumption—or some combination of such assumptions—one cares to make.

It is the Big Bang Force assumption that I would most like to explore here, because the other two have already been explored quite fully. The Big Bang must, Itself be a creative force. I say that because It arose out of Itself, *sui generis*. Nothing or no one preceded the physicists' big bang force, except incredibly condensed matter. Physicists apparently presume that the big bang force was created out of its own physical constituents, but I could be wrong. Apparently, the new Big Bang Itself is, according to my view, a creative Force whose expansion just keeps on doing whatever it is that It does, and that is the Force that began and still generates the evolution of the universe and of our little planet. Since the outcome of this evolution at present is races of peoples on earth, all with well-developed consciousnesses, I see no reason to assume that It does not have within Itself the ingredients that lead to consciousness, even though up to this point I have been assuming that It is not even aware, but merely terribly expressive. The evidence indicates that a necessary ingredient for consciousness is a nervous system specialized to the point where awareness of something specific at least is possible. That would apply to all of the animals, reptiles, birds, that is, all those with specialized senses. Then, if my son is any indication, consciousness occurs quite naturally—though a certain amount of language development may be necessary for it to arise in human beings. And we, we are made of the same substances that make up the rest of the earth; the distribution in us, however, is such that consciousness is present in us. But that same distribution of substances is also present in the Big Bang Force.

What is usually assumed, apparently, is that the composition that we are made up of is not to be present in the physical big bang force in the same fashion as in us. I find that a curious assumption: a creative force that continues flinging physical galaxies abroad that can have our kind of distribution of substances is what has been proposed. But because that force has not been found to have exactly our distribution of qualities—which are physical and mental and, depending upon how it is defined, spiritual—it has no awareness—none, none at all. And some of the people making that proposal do assume also the presence of a Deity—in addition. I suggest that in the new Big Bang Force that we join the two; surely the task of theorists is to unify what has been considered to be diverse. Newton joined the tides on earth and the motion of the moon in the heavens into one integrated system.

What stands in the way of such an integration with this issue is the prior conception or assumption that the big bang and its continuing force creating and recreating has an entirely physical origin. Our current cagegories simply do not allow us to think beyond that possibility. I say, let us, indeed, think beyond that possibility. All we need to do is to change one assumption, just one idea, and then the whole picture changes. Let us assume, as I am doing, that the new Big Bang Force arose from matter and spirit, in our limited conceptions, conjoined— pretty much as we are. That would sound very much like what the Deistic camp now holds, except that the two conceptions—the big bang and the Deistic have been kept in separate bins instead of being integrated into one unity. But suppose that the new Big Bang Force arose from some set of components that are *so different* from any we have even been able to *conceive* of that It does not display itself as we humans do. Apparently, It displayed itself only for physical measurement in this incredible big bang and in this essentially infinite universe—according to exactly how physicists and astronomers measure events. How It otherwise might display itself, we simply do not and cannot know. Remember, we cannot know Its nature. Might It not display itself at least in the registrations and the awarenesses of animals and in the registrations, awarenesses and consciousness of human beings? Perhaps its registrations prior to what we call life on earth were too minimal for our scientists even to grasp that they were there. One consequence of this way of thinking is that our deaths may not necessarily mean that people then enter into a state of nothingness. It certainly would seem as reasonable to assume that we rejoin the Source from which we spring—whatever That is. If you do not care to follow where my reasoning took me, perhaps you will concede that we do not and cannot know just what the categories are that make up the new Big Bang Force. Since that is the case, though our current conceptions posit an all physical source to the big bang, it could, as I said, as easily be posited that the source is beyond our categories as we know them currently, and probably forever. We could propose that the new Big Bang Force involves what we in our narrow categories refer to as physical and/or material and spiritual and/or mental all together. It is important to keep in mind that we are dealing with *assumptions* and not knowledge given once and for all as absolute and final fact. As Einstein once indicated, science is a process always subject to correction and doubt, and our current view of the big bang force is just the one physical scientists presently hold. It, accordingly, should be subjected to questions and doubts, since it is a conception merely currently espoused by persons.

I fear that a state that is neither physical/material nor mental/spiritual is one that is quite beyond our capacities at this time, but that should not deter us from entertaining such a possibility. And to do so is quite in the interest of the progress of science. A new Big Bang Force that can and has formed all of the stars and the galaxies could have thrown off our little planet and us without ever knowing it—especially if It is not conscious. It may just start things, and then It lets them take their course. It may not be what we call matter and it may not be what we call spirit—we'll never know. It is more than likely to be unknown, unknowable and beyond our finite categories. And our old matter is no longer matter anyway. As Fritjof Capra has said in the *Tau of Physics:* "at the subatomic level, matter does not exist with certainty at definite places, but rather shows 'tendencies to exist...'" If matter is moving in the direction of being nonmatter perhaps spirit can move in the direction of being less spiritual—and it, too, could become something beyond itself or beyond any of our current categories.

I mentioned one consequence of entertaining more open assumptions: that the idea of the outcome of death might necessitate a change for some. But one that is more germane to scientists, I believe, would be the consequences for our views of evolution. Darwin's theory of evolution provides us with a mechanistic or physical beginning and also such a continuing process. According to the assumption I have put forth a reevaluation of the nature of evolution would be required. If we were to assume that the new Big Bang Force is more than our current physical category provides, we would have less difficulty in conceiving of how animals with awarenesses could arise, for they would not be presumed to have arisen out of totally physical or mechanical matter. Instead, they would be presumed to have arisen from a source large enough in its conception to include the possibility of awareness arising. The same would be true of consciousness. We do not have to assume that it was a Being with consciousness who, with consciousness and intent, brought forth us with our consciousness. Instead, consciousness would arise simply because beings with awareness who also have our thalamo-cortical systems and our specialized receptors—eyes, ears, and such—simply will become aware of their own awarenesses when they reach something like the age of three years. A perfectly natural development would be presumed to occur in all creatures endowed as we are.

That natural development would probably involve at least one additional step between our conception of the physical and of our awarenesses as we human beings know them. Even a one cell animal such as the amoeba *registers* events. I am not prepared to accord to it our, or even a frog or a snake's awareness. The latter two must have some awarenesses because they have specialized receptors—eyes—which register, but also give them some of the differentiated qualities of the surrounding differentiated world. Amoebae lack these specialized receptors and so I suppose lack awarenesses, but they do register, for example, noxious stimuli. In this way, perhaps, the magnitude of the hiatus created by our assumption of purely physical/material events would be at least partly overcome. True, awareness is a state that arises somewhere along the line of phylogenetic development. But I am saying that that fact does not require that we also assume that prior to the development of awareness in the animal kingdom, there was no glimmering of awareness at least as registration anywhere, because *only our* physical world as currently defined existed. Frankly, we do not know that. But many scientists have been *assuming* that as if it were a fact. It is not fact, but assumption. If we change our assumptions about the nature of the originating source, we simply would no longer have to puzzle over how a being with consciousness could arise from materials that were entirely without awareness or consciousness. All we need is one cell that registers, and then accumulations of such cells into specialized units would give us awarenesses. And then we all know the rest of that story.

I am suggesting that the new Big Bang Force registers. Its registration is such as to have some kind of awareness, probably, given the prior assumption that it is not made entirely of what we currently call physical or material substance. Beyond that, and recall that that is only an assumption, we cannot know Its true nature. Of course, that assumption is subject to the prior assumption that the finite and the infinite are incomparable, and accordingly we cannot know the infinite, being ourselves finite. And that in turn involves a conclusion, based upon an assumption, that the new Big Bang Force, like God, is infinite rather than finite.

I have no way of knowing what Nicholas of Cusa, Cardinal of the Roman Catholic Church, would now have to say to all this. I must note, however, that he was a man who was very free in his examination of the assumptions of his time. Surely in examining the assumptions of our time he would still hold to the conclusion that "the sword, hate, envy . . . shall disappear, and all shall know . . .there is only one religion." Perhaps he would now conclude as I do, that we, the finite mortals that we are, can not know It. But we can conclude, as he did, that every human being is entitled to respect surrounding his or her deeply held spiritual beliefs. This respect for all truly religious worship, would, of course, have its basis in the disinterested interest that consciousness makes possible.

The remainder of this book demonstrates the presence of an objectively measured consciousness as an indicator of the spirit in spiritual humanism.

CHAPTER III

The Evolution of Consciousness

Since Newton there has been a notion that humanity on our earth, which had been the reigning center of the universe, was thereby dethroned. Accordingly, we became really nothings in the vast scheme of things. We became insignificant, ant-like creatures entirely peripheral to a huge physical system of which we are on the periphery anyway. Then with Darwin our special place on earth was usurped by the view that we are just animals in a long line of animals. Those views, both, I suggest, are unguarded. Though we are clearly not the center of the physical universe as we once thought we were, we are, indeed, the centers of the *spiritual* universe. Or, I should have said, we are, each of us, the center*s of the spiritual universes.* It is time for us to stop apologizing for our physical deficiencies, and pay attention to our spiritual *proficiencies.* Though we may arise from lower forms, as Darwin's theory tells us, our present status is such that we so far out stretch our nearest ancestors in the realm of the spirit, that we can be accorded a unique place again as the centers of the spiritual realms. Our spiritual capacities give rise to our critical importance in the larger scheme of the universe and the earth. For if it weren't for us, for us human beings, there would be no consciousness of a universe or of a Deity. The ideas of the universe and of a Deity arose only in the consciousness of human beings. All of the names for the entity that human beings have coined as God in recognition of a Deity would have gone unspoken, if it had not been for *homo sapiens.* And the conception of a universe and its big bang beginning would have gone totally unremarked were it not for us. Chimpanzees and gorillas may have preceeded us, as did many species of proto humans, but the total

Force that may have been inherent in the Big Bang had not yet, apparently, succeeded in creating in them the capacity for that consciousness that only the line of homo displays—at least in its present form—in us. For without our consciousness neither the universe nor the Godhead would ever have been acknowledgable.

Human consciousness was required for the postulation of a universe, for the proposed big bang, for the intestellar spaces, and the black holes—or even the idea of matter versus spirit. Human consciousness was also required for the proposal of a theory of evolution that placed us as akin to lower animals. The spirit that exists in us through our consciousness would never have been proposed as existent in a Being of a divine nature, if it were not for us and for the fact of our recognition of the spirit as well as of matter about two and one-half millenia ago. God owes humanity's consciousness for His existence. God and the universe only exist in the consciousness of human beings, and otherwise both would have remained not only unrecognized, but nonexistent, as they are nonexistent in chimpanzees. This view offers all of us an opportunity to reevaluate our place in nature, in the world and in the universe.

The Neanderthalers apparently came close to what we are, but failed to survive. On what grounds they failed to survive, we really do not know. We would have to depend entirely upon speculation which really offers no help for understanding how we came to be, because it is only after the fact that Darwinian theory could *try* to explain the disappearance of the Neanderthalers. And, perhaps, isn't it even quite likely that we too are only intermediate creatures on the way to becoming the higher spiritual beings that our race may yet someday become? We do not know, and we cannot know. But even now we do, indeed, know that we have the quality of the spirit that the total Force I assume may be inherent in the Big Bang may have in unparalleled abundance. *We do have that spiritual capacity for consciousness of a universe and a Deity.* And that means that we have responsibilities to that side of ourselves—our consciousness of the spirit that has been and is being lost in our secular age. Everyone acknowledges that we have a physical and material side. But we also have a spiritual side.

That side has too often remained undeveloped; it exists even now, perhaps, merely in an embryonic state.

The Neanderthaler's spiritual side is evident in the flowers they placed on the graves of their dead. Some cognizance, or at least some sense of some spirit beyond matter is evident there. In the history of humanity this evidence of the spirit has been enshrined in the various religions. How confused these spiritual expressions often were should be no surprise given the complex nature of what we still refer to as our psycho-bio-physical constitutions. The terms *psychobiological, psychophysical, and psychosomatic* demonstrate the split natures of our beings. It is, or should be, no surprise then that our spiritual life has been and still is embedded in obscurity, ambiguity, and anonymity. And there have even been denials that there is such a spirit by those who see the spiritual sides of our beings and consciousness itself as mere epiphenomena. Consciousness is no epiphenomenon. And it seems to me that the spiritual nature of humanity arises, or at least rises to awareness, from that consciousness that is everywhere present in human beings. (That that consciousness is also a function of the nature of our cerebral cortices, I hope it is understood, I take for granted.) But given the probability that we cannot know whatever Deity there might be, a new approach to humanity's spiritual life is called for—I think, demanded. It is time that we stopped our religious and secular bickering and set forth our task in the light of our undoubted consciousness of humanity's spiritual nature.

When anthropologists speculate on the earliest human creatures and how they lived, they always find there some belief in spiritual beings beyond themselves. What I am suggesting is that this sense of the Spirit, out there, arises from our own personal sense of enspiritedness and consciousness within us. I believe that this quality that has gone by the name of *spirit* arises from the sense that all of us have of a something that animates us and is different from and beyond our bodily experiences. That spirit is what comes to its fullest estate in human consciousness. We are animated beings—though we may no longer be so when we are brain dead—but more of that later. This animation is evident even in the newborn infant. But beyond that animation infants less than three days-old demonstrate more interest when the surrounding color changes than when it remains the same. The change in the color of the surround is a physical event in our current conceptions. The infant is a physical-physiological organism in our current conceptions. From whence does the change in interest derive? From the physical and the physiological, of course, but those are not all. They are necessary, but they are not enough to account for the change in *interest*. Does the infant contribute nothing? I say that the infant contributes a great deal: Her *personal interest!* The fact that the study involved a group of infants does not obviate the fact that the group finding was necessarily based upon each infant's individual interest in the change in color. The individual infant is here disclosing his individual *psychological interest*. I see personal and individual interests as the essence of what is psychological as differentiated from the physical and biological or physiological.

The external physical change in light waves or photons, the physiological change received by the retina of the eye, and, of course, its components in the cerebral cortex, are necessary conditions for the observed changes in the awarenesses of the infants to occur. The sufficient condition, what ultimately *causes* the reaction to occur, is an infant whose individual expressive nature is in readiness to respond to the changes. That is the psychological outcome of the necessarily physical and physiological activity. But each infant has to contribute expressively out of its meaning for him or her for the psychological awareness and increased interest to occur. This expressivity arises from an intact cerebral cortex properly stimulated at the retina of the eye by a physical change in the external environment. The outcome is the individual psychological experiencing of an awareness of a change in color by each infant.

Not enough attention has been paid to the sequence I just outlined. Of course, it is a complicated sequence and, I believe, that that is why people have overlooked it. Indeed, there have even been psychologists who believed we could ignore that whole sequence and deal simply with the overt behavioral outcome. Naturally, that would also leave out any sense of the spirit within each one of us.

The theorizing, for that is what it was, a theory out of the consciousness of the theorist, whose own consciousness clearly went far beyond what his theoretical bent was able to conceive. It was just wrong headed. The spirit of the theorist went beyond what he wished to acknowledge theoretically. Such theorizing itself arises from psychological experiencings of awarenesses for which the theory could never have given an account. Theorizing arises out of that same expressive psychological awareness that was evidenced in the infants' awarenesses of the change in color. But such theorizing involves much more than expressivity, though that is, of course, there.

Theorizing involves both consciousness and a personal sense of what is important enough to spend one's thought and consciousness upon for a sustained period of time. Einstein's special theory of relativity occupied his major, if not his sole, interest and commitment for seven long years. The outcome was, of course, a theory, a *symbolic conception* of the nature of moving things in the physical universe. He did not merely describe the real world or universe, but put in place of that real world, an idea of the world and the universe whose predictions about events in the real world came close enough to give credence to the theory. Einstein's theory was an idealized statement of physical nature, not a factual statement of it.

Idealizations are akin to what I have been refering to as spirit; they emanate from consciousness. Idealizations arise out of our human capacity to symbolize, and to symbolize to ourselves in consciousness through our imagination events that are impossible to fulfill in reality. Our sense of a spiritual life is at least in part an outcome of such imaginative, idealizing activities. We are all equipped with these propensities. The evidence for this statement resides even in the views of cynics, for what they espouse are not actual circumstances, but idealized conditions, rather than real ones. The conditions under which cynicism arises are ideal because they are not descriptions of realities, but of possibilities which are in fact not present to the senses of the cynic. They reside only in his rarified consciousness. The fact that it is a negative view of possibilities does not detract from the basic fact that it is a symbolic way of representing a world that does not really exist.

Cynics adhere to an ideal world, not the real one. And their ideal world arises out of the spirit that is evident in symbolic idealizations in human consciousness. And, then they deny the possibility of spiritual events arising within themselves even, as they set forth a view of human events that is only in part true, and is beyond the facts. They exaggerate.

Darwin was no cynic, of course, quite the contrary. He was a positive thinking person, but he believed that he was describing the origin and the development of humanity by proposing to account only for its physical and physiological side. Since we cannot really know the nature of our origins once we reject the usual categories with which we have been presented historically, a new and broadened theory of the evolution of humanity is in order. Basing evolution on the simplistic dichotomy of physical as real and the spirit as unreal has to mean that it is at best sadly incomplete. The theory is incomplete, because we just do not know that that dichotomy truly describes the total reality. Simply because our physical and biological scientists have restricted themselves to physical-physiological conceptions in their theory of the evolution of the species does not make it so. Let's begin again. That is what I intend to do here even though I have to acknowledge that I sadly lack the ability to formulate a verbal concept which can integrate the physical and the spiritual. I hope, however, that you will keep in mind that that should be the ultimate aim, and perhaps should be the ultimate aim of all of us, even though I fail to achieve it here.

I have little quarrel with the notion that the rocks and mountains of the earth evolved with little of the spirit very evident in them. However, as Stephen Jay Gould makes very clear in "Cordelia's Dilemma," though he did not have in mind what I am suggesting here, the fact of negative results does not mean that something is non existent. The fact that what I am calling spirit was not evident before the advent of highly developed creatures, does not mean that it was then, and had always been, non existent. Perhaps the fact that our measures are all physical ones precluded anything but physical events from being recorded.

Remember that I am only using the term *spirit* because I have not been able to specifiy that more general concept that would include both matter and spirit in one term. Consequently, that does not mean as current evolutionary theory has it, that something of the spirit wasn't there all along. It simply was not prominently enough in evidence, with the limited means and concepts at our disposal, to prove its existence to scientists whose only orientation was to physically measured events. But, at any rate, along the eons long-line of time a one-celled organism arose. It arose apparently as a mutation. I do not want to presume that consciousness thereby also arose—not at all. But if that organism were anything like the modern amoeba, and there is reason to believe that it was, then that organism, like the amoeba, was capable of registering external stimulation. By the way, the theory of evolution does not really account for mutations, and yet some well-known current theorists, Gould among them, do consider that the the events in evolution show saltatory leaps rather than a total continuity. Where the rocks register only by being worn away by rushing water or by being chipped by a larger moving rock, and thereby register only in the most minimal fashion, one celled organisms register and to some extent also retain that registration. If registration can be assumed to be an indication of a modest amount of the spirit at work beyond matter, then it also can, at the very least, be proposed, just proposed, as existent certainly from the very beginning of the Big Bang.

Our cells, of course, register too. We consist of millions of such cells, but a cell is a cell, and registration is something that all cells do, and they register more than rocks do. Instead of raising the question, as has been the case: How can we account for consciousness arising from physical-physiological sources? we can assert that just as the infant registered the change in the surrounding color as a prelude to what would some day be consciousness, so too evolutionarily speaking, is the registering of the one-celled being and even the rock, on the way to becoming a human being with awarenesses and consciousness. Though the single cell has only achieved registration at this point in its evolutionary development, we know that with a sufficient conglomeration of such cells of a specialized kind there will eventually be awareness, and, with our thalamo-cortical systems, even consciousness in addition to registration and awareness.

Consciousness is a late comer in ontogenetic life and also, I believe, in phylogenetic existence. Consciousness, however, arises not as something entirely new out of a physical-physiological being devoid of anything like the spirit, but out of beings that register. That statement proposes, of course, what is only an assumption. Registration requires a responsiveness that is at the lowest level of expressivity. But registration in the amoeba, unlike the slow and minimal, but still a kind of registration effect of running water over rocks, indicates a considerable level of expressivity. The amoeba expresses itself by rejecting noxious materials, for example. This expressivity could be evidence of a smidgen of the spirit which had entered the cell in such a fashion that even the most hide-bound non believer might acknowledge it as more than merely its physical-chemical-physiological constituents. Remember, the idea that there is no spirit anywhere is a concept raised by humanity, just as that there is spirit everywhere is also one so raised—both new and so ancient as it is— by humanity. The Big Bang was certainly expressive! We have, of course, been conceiving of that as a purely physical-chemical event, but we do not know that that is truly the case. We have assumed it. I believe that it is merely a presumption. It is, I believe, an example of what Alfred North Whitehead has called the "unguardedness" of science. Science, he indicated is unguarded to the extent that it has unstated assumptions at work within its theories.

Though physicists no doubt would be willing to state explicitly their physical assumption, it is unguarded of them to ignore the possibility that their physical assumption may be only part of the truth, or even a falsehood. If we take the fact of expression as being more responsive and therefore more unlike most so-called inorganic matter, such as rocks and gravel, we could assume that something nonphysical, neither organic nor inorganic, but beyond both, is at work in the Big Bang. For want of a better term, I am calling it Spirit—though I know that that term is probably not at all adequate to its reality. I am assuming that something of what we think of vaguely as spirit was present when the Big Bang occurred. Furthermore, it could well have been the case that the Spirit, or spirit, was integral to the occurence of the Big Bang. We cannot know that it was, of course; similarly, we cannot know that it was not. We would not know that something of the spirit was present, because the Spirit is, or may be, immeasurable in physicist-astronomer terms. It was easier and simpler, especially for Western philosophers and scientists, to place the Big Bang into a category known since approximately six hundred BC, as material or as physical.

Perhaps the assumption that a Spirit was present and even a part of the Big Bang is an unwarranted assumption. Since that could be the case, I'll offer an alternative. Let's assume that the Spirit was not expressed along with the Big Bang. Instead, let us assume that the spirited quality remained unexpressed, and unacknowledged and unacknowledgeable by us, until the evolution of organic matter. And then the recognizable expression of a spirited quality had reached the point in evolution when something of that larger Spirit, which had been present all along, was finally revealed. No intent need be presumed to have occurred in all of this, but our factual observations do indicate that evolution does occur as a fact. I am not quarreling with the facts of evolution; I am, though, indeed, quarreling with Darwin's *theory* of evolution. And I am especially quarreling with its present-day formulations that have tied it to a Mendelian mathematical formula that has been interpreted as evolution on the basis of chance. Darwin did not believe that evolution operated on a chance basis. He even said:

> I have hitherto sometimes spoken as if the variations—so common and multiform with organic beings under domestication, and to a lesser degree with those under nature—were due to chance. This, of course, is a wholly incorrect expression, but it serves to acknowledge plainly our ignorance of the
> cause of each particular variation.

The Mendelian mathematical ratio not only does not constrain us to the assumption that chance is at work, but opposes that view. The same is true for the randomness that Stephen J. Gould preferred in *Hens Teeth and Horse's Toes*, as the basis for genetic inheritance. Perhaps it is merely because evolution has heretofore only been concerned with physical and, perhaps, physiological evolution that that seems to be the case.

The evolution of whatever the Totality was, or at least might have been, that made up the Big Bang could have included a Spiritual quality that was overlooked for the so palpable physical quality that was so obvious and, perhaps more important for our history and civilization: It was measurable! The Spirit that I am proposing may have been immeasurable, to use Patricia F. Carini's apt phrase in her "Images and Immeasurables," (but employed in a different context) by which she meant not not measured yet, and not merely unmeasurable, but immeasurable—never to be measured! The Spirit is beyond measurement; it is immeasurable now, and, I believe, will be immeasurable forever. But organic beings in the form of amoebae, I propose, have a smidgen of that other spirit—the one that is evident in their registrations. The fact that they register events is my evidence for assuming that they do have an aspect of spirit. At the same time I am fully aware that the spirit, which I suggest as a counterpart to matter, is only a poor relation to what that overarching concept that would include matter and Spirit in one term would actually be like.

Instead of worrying about how it is possible for life to arise from inorganic matter, we now have the new problem of trying to understand how it is possible for the spirit, out of a totality, that includes our physical and spiritual in one, to have taken so many millenia to be expressed in a form that is finally interpretable as what it is: A spiritual quality. One could assume, that a spiritual or Spiritual component evolved along side of, or intermingled with, the physical one. I think that it has been the narrowness of our Western conceptions that has prevented us from considering that assumption. Alternatively, I believe that since we do not know the nature of whatever that was that might have been there all along, It simply might not have known how to express Itself in a form we could understand. We don't have to presume that it is either all powerful or all knowing, you know.

Since the expression of the Big Bang has been treated as if it were purely a physical event, and because Spirit is immeasurable, we may now well wonder what took *us* so long to see the obvious. I believe that it was the prior assumption that matter was all that was real, and spirit or the Spirit was merely a mistaken notion of primitive peoples. Since anthropology began we have assumed that the earliest humans were primitives who projected spirits into inorganic materials. But that was merely further evidence, I suggest, of the physical assumption at work. It has been that physical assumption that has held us in thrall. The Spirit may have been present all along, but we were looking in the wrong direction. We were looking only through physicalist eyes. The right direction to have looked would be where there is major evidence for it—even if it has not been going by that name. The human psyche is the direction toward which we must look for evidence of the human spirit which may be the only evidence that we have of the Spirit that I am suggesting may have evolved along with the physical.

Consciousness, awareness of our own awarenesses, however, is probably only as old as the Neanderthalers—that means, perhaps, 100,000 years. Perhaps it is older, or is not that old; maybe it arose only with *homo sapiens*. Before that there existed between registration and consciousness a long history of organisms that shared with us the capacity for awareness. Awareness was present in the two day-old infants who responded expressively to the change in the color of the surround. Awareness, when it is not used so broadly as to be synonymous with consciousness, refers to an awareness of something or of some thing or things. Awareness of something differs both from consciousness and from conscious. Conscious, without the *ness*, usually refers to the physical state of not being knocked out, of not being comatose. For comatose we use the term unconscious. Awareness, as I am using the term, refers to something relatively specific. Amoebae, according to my definition, do not have enough specificity in their receptor systems to have awarenesses. Their responses are entirely vague and global because they have no specialized receptors, not even taste and smell, much less the highly differentiated eyes and ears that we have. Awareness of some quality or of some thing requires specialized receptors. Clams, molusks and such-like creatures have very minimal specialized senses. They register, of course, and something perhaps more than that, because there is some differentiation of their cells, but their awarenesses would be very vague if present at all. The amphibians have more specialized receptors, and, they also have an increased neocortex; it is the combination of these two—specialized receptors and the neocortex—which allow for more and more differentiated awarenesses to arise. Phylogentically, the progenitors of the human race on its spiritual side have moved from registration to awareness. Then, finally, in *homo sapiens* certainly, humanity has moved to consciousness. The evolution of that spirit can been seen as paralleling the evolution of the physical world.

What, then, are we to think of this other evolution, this new evolution that includes the spirit as well as the physical? Darwin's basic theory was extremely simple. Accepting the observation that organisms at the lower levels are oversupplied, he invoked Malthus' theory that there would be a shortage of available food, for example, due to the overpopulation, and therefore he proposed a struggle among the plethora of species for survival. Then those species which are adaptable enough in the struggle to survive will adapt, and they will accordingly survive. And, the theory tells us, it is those who adapted who have survived. I have always thought that Darwin's theory should have been applied to species and not within species, so my understanding is that the species who are currently in existence, have survived because they adapted in the struggle for existence. Though apparently that may not altogether account for the disappearance of the dinosaurs or the Neanderthalers. As I have indicated, Darwin's was a theory about physical and physiological evolution—not the evolution of our totality which would have to include the evolution of consciousness from registrations and awarenesses.

Darwin's theory of evolution is a practical theory. By that I mean that it was intended to account for what is presently actually in existence in the world as physical bodies. But we are not just physical bodies; we are beings of the spirit as well. Some Darwinians presume that consciousness must have had an adaptive function, else it would not have arisen. Following Darwin's practical bent they assume that consciousness, along with the language to which it is related, allowed human beings to hunt more efficiently, and that caused them to survive over other species. In presuming such a view, for it is a presumption, they overlook entirely the spiritual side of human development. The art displayed in all of those caves of which we have become aware, they accordingly interpret as having some practical use for the hunt. There is no warrant at all for such a *presumption*—except the prior assumptions that only a material and physical evolution have taken place. I say that the arts displayed in those caves are a function of the evolution of the human spirit! The arts and the religions, both indicating the aspirations of human beings beyond practicalities, along with science, are the true evidences of the human spirit at work. And all of these human aspirations involve not only registrations and awareness, but consciousness, and even, perhaps, that new level of the consciousness of our own consciousness. We can even reflect upon what enters into our reflective processes and make artistic, scientific, religious, and spiritual decisions based upon that very complex level of consciousness. That is where the evolution of consciousness has brought us human beings.

That is my theory, or nontheory, of evolution. I cannot place my current formulation into the neat categories of Darwin's for two reasons. Evolution of the complex totality of our humanity was not simply physical, I suggest, and accordingly would require a more complex formulation. Moreover, that more complex formulation might involve the spiritual realm which in the larger sense is immeasurable—so no formulation would ever be able to be simple, as simple as his, even allied with the Mendelian formula, ever again. And perhaps no formulation will ever be satisfactory no matter how complex a formulation it may be, for there are not only the events that we do not know, but perhaps as well those that can never be known. I'll do my best in the next chapter to indicate how we might proceed, but it isn't neat, and it may not be at all satisfactory to the scientific world—at least to the world of the biological and physical sciences—nor to the world of religious doctrines.

CHAPTER IV

Physics and the Science of Anthropomorphic Optics

Psychologists have too often come to the conclusion that psychology is dependent upon physics rather than that physics is dependent upon psychology. That view arose, I believe, because we are dependent upon the physical world in several ways. We have to cope with it successfully for our physical survival and well-being. Then, the physical world is present to our five senses, and the psychological world is largely unavailable through the senses. It may also be thought to be private rather than public as the physical world is acknowledged to be. It is also the case that the split between physical and mental, though it took many millenia until the early Greek philosophers formulated that split, was one that satisfied the clear headed Greeks and all of the remainder of us who appreciate clarity. The split is with us still. That the physical was palpable to all, and the mental was not, seemed also to give the physical its priority. We psychologists even have to consider the *physical* measurement of the events we study in our laboratories, if we are to arrive at psychological facts that are scientific.

But none of these several reasons, as real as they are, require that we place *physics*—a science created by human beings—as prior to our individual psychological functioning. Psychologically, babies even at birth are aware of and respond to changes in their surroundings. Our psychological awarenesses arose long before we had an awareness of physical things apart from us. Yes, physics as a science was also created long before psychology had scientific pretensions. However, a science created by human beings to examine and theorize about physical phenomena comes under the rubrics of psychological functions, for all human awarenesses are the province of psychology. And physics arose out of the awarenesses and consciousness of human beings, of physicists. Physics, accordingly, does not reside in a privileged position vis a vis psychology. In fact, since the creation of physics was conducted by the psychological processes of human beings, it makes much more sense to acknowledge the priority of psychology in the construction of the science of physics. That is the strange premise, strange that is, to current common sense, upon which this chapter is based.

In *The Emperor's New Mind,* and similarly, in his more recent book, *Shadows of the Mind,* Roger Penrose argues powerfully that it is our consciousness that prevents an acceptance of the strong artificial intelligence (SAI) position. The advocates of SAI suggest that complicated computers will be able to duplicate all of the complex human activities, even those that we know as consciousness, or as a function of consciousness. Penrose writes:

> Consciousness seems to me to be such an important phenomenon that I simply cannot believe that it is something just 'accidentally' conjured up by a complicated computation. It is the phenomenon whereby the universe's very existence is made known. . . .
>
> It is only the phenomenon of consciousness that can conjure a putative 'theoretical' universe into actual existence!

It is, indeed, consciousness through which "the universe's very existence is made known." That is, it is consciousness through which their "'theoretical' universe," or even our less theoretical physical world exists. And though he does not make the distinctions between awareness and consciousness that I do, and overlooks registrations entirely, he does display in his examples some sense of the distinction

I make between awareness and consciousness. Consequently, all of his statements above are ones with which I fully agree.

But he also cites a delemma within which he is caught that is not present by beginning with psychology rather than by beginning with physics. He puts it this way:

> In my own arguments I have tried to support this view that there must indeed be something essential that is missing from any purely computational picture. Yet I hold also to the hope that it is through science and mathematics that some profound advances in the understanding of mind must eventually come to light.

Penrose, however, means by 'science' physical science. I suggest that it has to be a science, but a psychological one which will advance our knowledge of the role of "mind," or consciousness, not a physicist's one. His "hope," I believe, will have to remain unfulfilled, because registrations, awarenesses, and consciousness, *all*, are missing entirely from the physicists' theoretical universe. The three human states of registration, awareness, and consciousness are touched by, and the last even suffused by, I suggest, the spirit of humanity. A different premise than a physical one is better able to solve Penrose's delemma.

In this chapter Penrose's delemma is solved through a scientific theory of perception, the theory of anthropomorphic optics in which I attribute human qualities even to our eyes. As important as the brain as a physical, physiological, or neurological organ is, the solution to the role of consciousness in human conduct has to rest upon psychological premises and processes from a psychological theory, and not from physical ones. The immense gaps that separate the physics, the physiology, and the neurology of the brain from understanding human consciousness is serious enough. But that physical orientation overlooks entirely the basic problem facing psychology that simply cannot be addressed by physics. It is this: *Why do people act as they do?*

Physics has never given, does not give, and, I believe cannot give, an answer to that question. Physics tells us how and why objects move, and the tides change, and it even tells how human bodies in free fall accelerate, but it otherwise does not tell us why people act as they do. It has never even studied the actions of people as a prelude to explaining them. *Consciousness* has a role to play in the answer to why we act as we do, but it is not always central to that question. In a like fashion for psychology the issue is not whether SAI can account for human thinking or for consciousness—and I believe that Penrose is right that it cannot—but for psychology the basic question is: *Why do we act as we do?* Both thinking and consciousness have a role to play in the answer to psychology's question. Sometimes they are central, but sometimes they are not. But the enterprise from a physicist's position, or an SAI one, misses the mark entirely. By focussing on thinking and consciousness instead of upon why we act as we do, they focus on a peripheral rather than a central issue. The psychological theory I sketch below provides the basis for that explanation of human actions. Then both thinking and consciousness will, and do, find their proper places as ancillary to the major task of psychology. Just as physics answers the question, why do things move as they do? Psychology has to answer the question: Why do people act as they do? The full answer will occupy this chapter and Chapter V.

I believe Penrose and the AI—strong or weak—advocates have approached the issue of consciousness as central because they see the issues in laymen's terms rather from a professional, scientific psychologist's point of view. Neither of them have studied thinking; they are at best amateurs in that enterprise. The strong AI advocates have *presumed* that thinking is essentially what their computers do. It is not.

A subtler difference between physics and psychology also needs to be acknowledged before the theory can be presented. Physical theories account for the large scale factual movements such as the tides on earth, the phases of the moon, the movements of the planets, and even the events in remote outer space. They tell us why things move as they do in the larger physical world. They also tell us that they can account for the fall of leaf that swirls in the autumn breeze—

even though any predictions that they might make would never be correct. They cannot tell us where a leaf caught in a breeze will fall or when it will fall, or even once fallen, whether it will stay on the ground. But we believe that they have the theory to account for the falling leaf, even though in such an instance they cannot predict it directly as they can the moon and the tides. They prove their theory by placing the leaf in a vacuum, and lo, it falls exactly where and at the time that they predicted it would. Psychologists have been thinking that a psychological theory would have to be like the theories that account for the motions of the planets, the stars, and the other events in outer space. They have assumed that psychology must account *directly* for the everyday actions of people as they carry on the complex activities of their daily lives. I suggest that that view presumes a likeness to astronomy, rather than to the vacuum of the physicists. That astronomical model cannot be applied to a psychologicial explanation of our everyday human actions. Instead, I suggest that the test of a psychological theory is as a laboratory science, just as physics is when it uses a vacuum to demonstate its mastery over the fall of a leaf from the tree. The physicist knows that he cannot tell us where or when the leaf will fall even on a reasonably calm day. To prove his theory he takes us into his laboratory and places the leaf in a vacuum; then and only then can he predict where and when the leaf will reach the ground. Their theory is tested under the controlled conditions of a vacuum. But we all acknowledge from that demonstration that they do have the explanation for the fall of the leaves in the autumn.

Psychology is comparable to the latter, to the laboratory side of physics only. I suggest three factors, formally expressed as the three axioms of anthropomorphic optics, to account for the visual qualities perceived by persons. Then these perceptions, or awarenesses more generally, are proposed in the following chapter as the explanation for our actions. A spirited expressivity, I suggested earlier, is a characteristic of infants. I see it also as a characteristic of human awarenesses in general. We express verbally in sentences, in phrases, in emotional expostulations; we express by moving, our bodies, our limbs and our facial muscles; we express ourselves through artistic works; we express our emotions willy nilly; and we express our feelings that arise from our values. Every movement we make is a human expression; such movements are ubiquitous in us. To see the operation of psychology in a way that is comparable to the physicist's problem of predicting the fall of a leaf in a breeze is simply to adapt those expressive individual experiences we have during our everyday lives to a laboratory setting. Even when we merely look at a person, we experience not the bare physical-physiological imprint upon our senses, though that is, of course, registered, but we experience the meaning of what we see. What is important about our perceptions is whether we not only *register*, but recognize the person or thing before us. Recognition is registration and awareness on the reception side, but it involves our expressive natures as well, because our nervous system responds expressively. We experience a meaning that occurs within us in every act of awareness. That meaning may involve what the person means to us, recognized or unrecognized, and how we feel about her, to mention just a few considerations. We experience an impression of the person: We are aware that we like or dislike her, feel antipathy toward or interest in her. These impressions occur essentially instantaneously. We always go far beyond the physical-physiological impression with our enspirited individual expression of her meaning for us. These events in our daily lives are too complex, too fleeting, and too ephemeral to measure. However, in laboratory experiments, which are comparable to the leaf in a physical vacuum, we can demonstrate the occurence of that spirited expressivity in a group of adults as a measurable fact. That expressivity is one of three factors in the theory of anthropomorphic optics.

A brief consideration of the brain is necessary at this point. The cerebral cortex of the brain is divided by a fissure which separates the anterior, or front edge of the sensory portion of the parietal lobes, from the posterior, or back edge of the motor portion of the frontal lobes. The fissure is about one-third of the way back from the front of the brain and gives rise to a tonic state in the organism, a kind of organic alertness, an ongoing state that is responsive to sensory or to motoric outputs. Besides the motor portion of the frontal lobes and sensory portion of the parietal lobe there is, for our purposes, the occipital lobe (seeing) at the rear of the brain. The movements of the body to some extent inhibit the sensory expressions, and strong sensory inputs somewhat inhibit expressive movements, but expressive surroundings—smiling at an infant—can bring out expressive movements in that infant—waving the arms and legs. The sensory and the motor inputs give rise to changes in awarenesses and to changes in movements respectively. In the laboratory the ongoing tonic state can be manipulated so that motoric or sensory-perceptual expressions can be the outcome. A series of experiments demonstrated, for example, that accelerating the immobilized human body from zero to sixty miles per hour in ten seconds caused the awareness of the size of a simple circle of light to appear larger (or nearer). The increased cerebellar activity brought on by the powerful acceleration caused the awarenesses of a group of observers to be *expressed* as a change in that visual sensory awareness or perception. The expressivity of the cerebral cortex accordingly became a measured scientific fact which confirms one axiom of the theory. It is evidence such as this which indicates that widely separated areas of the brain must operate together all of the time.

Expressivity, then, occurs not only in daily life but also under the measurable conditions of a laboratory, and I suggest that it is one indication of an *enspirited* quality in human beings.

Laboratory demonstrations of the reciprocal role of sensory and motoric expressions are not unusual, but they have not often been focussed upon despite the ubiquitousness of expressivity in everyday life. When overt physical expressivity is magnified, for example, waving the arms about in large swinging movements, autokinetic motions (the apparent movements of a stationary light in darkness) decrease. Here the motoric expressivity inhibited the perceptual expressivity. At the opposite end it has been shown that immobilizing each persons' head allows each one to be aware of small and brief movements visually of which they had otherwise remained unaware. These examples demonstrate the measurable amounts of the expressivity of the intact cerebral cortices whose effects are so much in evidence in our everyday lives. Without intact cerebral cortices, however, the projection of movement that is a normal function of the intact brain does not occur. Brain damaged boys, for example, when presented briefly with a drawing of a man with one foot in the air see the man as stopped, as arrested, as not moving; normal boys perceive the man as walking—just caught momentarily in the continuous act of taking a step, but as part of an ongoing movement. The degree of expressivity and thus of enspiritedness differs in the two groups of boys. Our *projection of liveliness* into the world around us is part of our intact human cerebral cortices that come out in an enspirited expressivity. These ordinary human projections of an awareness of motion on the dead physical world are evidences, I suggest, of something of the spirit at work in all human beings. It is our enspirited natures which *project* these awarenesses of movements that are not physically there at all. These projections when added to by the other two components of the theory are what lay the basis for imagination.

That strong expressive spirit is lacking in the lower animals. Though they, as is the frog, for example, are overwhelmingly responsive to real motions, they have not the developed expressivity that is so strong in us—when our cerebral cortices are undamaged—that is. A frog is unable to inhibit its response to an actual movement, and thus will strike at a moving pin, and continue to strike at it even though it receives no food from it, and in the process has reduced its tongue to shreds. Yet the frog is receptive and aware of movements. It does not have consciousness, however. Its receptivity, awareness, and expressivity are at a lower level only. The human spirit is *lacking*. Whether chimpanzees and gorillas share this aspect of expressivity with us, though unknown, is I think likely, because its physical location in the brain is an essential aspect of its operation.

To examine other human qualities as laboratory phenomena it is necessary to consider briefly, and as simply as possible, other aspects of the nature of the brain in relation to human awarenesses. We share with the higher animals an ancient limbic system deep in the brain that is centrally related to the survival of the organism. To recognize dangerous situations, and when attacked to respond by struggling to survive, appears to be a quality of essentially all sentient beings. But all of them do not have a limbic system such as we and the higher animals do have. What this means is that there must be qualities in perception that are a function of the limbic system, since we have to see, or perceive the nature of the situation before we can judge it to be dangerous to life. Central to such percepts are the relations among a set, or among sets of events. In life we see the relations among the parts of a complex situation and grasp its meaning immediately as innocuous or dangerous. Sometimes we are mistaken about the reality of the threat and respond as if the threat were real. And, of course, in some situations the threat is real. It is the limbic system which is basic to such fears and emotional feelings of danger which are so important for our survival. We are all accustomed to such strong emotional reactions, and these emotions are central in *motivating* us to act. All of these emotional reactions arise from the ancient limbic system which we especially share with monkeys, gorillas, and chimpanzees.

Strong feelings about survival are thus engaged through our and their limbic systems. But our physical survival is not always at the forefront of our everyday awarenesses, as it may well be for those others in their searches for physical survival. We are not even constantly concerned about our physical survivial, for as Alfred North Whitehead has said of us in his *Modes of Thought*, "the life aim at survival is modified into the human aim at survival for diversified worthwhile experience." Our powerful frontal lobes change the arousal of the limbic system, so that our aims are greatly modified compared to those other animals. We thus have strong *feelings* about many things that do *not* compel them, the arts, ethics and morals, justice and human welfare in general, rather than the merely raw emotional reactions that are a function of the limbic system. All such strong emotional drives are modified in us by the effects of the frontal lobes on the ancient limbic system. Our emotional reactions can in this way be turned into *feelings about the value* of something by our reflective processes in consciousness.

In the laboratory we find counterparts to these concerns about how phenomena directly *pertain* to the person's life in how two events out there may *pertain to one another*. How things belong together or pertain can be studied in the laboratory as an attenuated aspect of how things and people pertain to us in everyday life. In the laboratory *appurtenance* does not involve what we care deeply about, what we value, or what matters to us in everyday life. Though appurtenance is what is centrally involved in our struggles for our physical survival, it also involves how any two events out there pertain to one another in our experience of them, just as an event out there and our survival would pertain. Instead of what pertains directly to us and matters to us, as the events do in everyday life, how objects pertain to one another in the laboratory allow us to investigate modifications of those important relations. There how those phenomena pertain to one another uncomplicated by emotionality can be studied. And then we can apply what we find there to what pertains to us in living our daily lives.

The human spirit is, I believe, comprised as an intricate complex of three basic factors. The first one is *expressivity* and the second is *appurtenance*, how things *pertain* to us, or to one another. The third factor is the *symbolizing* of all of our experiences by the operation of the frontal lobes upon the rest of the brain. All of these are probably also affected by Gerald M. Edelman's "reentrant circuits" which he describes in *Bright Air, Brilliant Fire*. I'll return to these after presenting the effects of appurtenance as phenomena in laboratory settings.

In the laboratory appurtenance is studied in the relations of two events to one another. A *Scientific American* article many years ago demonstrated that an orange circle could be changed into a brown circle when the surrounding light became extremely bright. When the orange circle pertained to an ordinary background the observers were aware of it as an orange circle; when the center pertained to a very bright outline surrounding it, the observers became aware of it as a brown circle. The same occurence results in our everyday light as the moon in the day time appears white against the blue sky, but we are aware of it as a luminous orb when it is surrounded by darkness. Several of the well-known geometrical illusions have also been shown to lose their illusory quality when their two parts are separated in depth or in time. The depth or time separation causes the illusion that occurs when the two pertain to one another, no longer to pertain, and their illusory quality disappears. The awarenesses of the motion of a single red light traveling vertically up and down, can be so entrained by two blue lights—one above and one below the red light, but moving horizontally—that there is a change in the physically vertical movement of the red light into an awareness of a diagonal motion. This change only occurs, however, when the blue lights and the red light are at the same distance. When the red light is in front of the blue lights, the red light reverts to its perceived actual, or physical, vertical motion.

The third factor, that of *symbolizing* events—to present and represent events to ourselves reflectively—the third axiom, is relevant also to this effect of appurtenance on the angle of movement of the red light described above. In one part of the above experiment, when the blue lights and the red light were not at the same depth (the set of blue lights was presented farther away), and consequently the blue lights had *no* effect on the vertical motion of the red light. However, when the observers were asked merely *to pay attention* to the blue lights farther away, but with their eyes still *physically focussed* on the red light nearby, the result was changed to a perceived partial diagonal—forty-five percent of the earlier diagonal—movement! The actual *physical vertical* motion of the red light was perceived as nearly half of the diagonal motion on the basis of *consciousness* alone! For it was consciousness alone which countermanded the effect of the *physical-physiological* focus on the red light to produce the approximately forty-five percent of the diagonal motion that appurtenance had *physically* enforced. That physical focus should have resulted in a vertical motion, but the vertical path was overcome by the mere focus in *consciousnsess* on the blue lights! That means that the instructions, merely asking the observers to symbolize, that is, to represent to themselves in consciousness, the centrality of the far blue lights even though they were physically fixated on the near red light, had a powerful effect on the awareness of the angle of the motion. The third factor—symbolizing that awareness only in *consciousness*—had a *measurable* effect on the physical operation of appurtenance. An aspect of the effect of consciousness on a physical event was here measured! Though all three axioms contribute to the spirit in spiritual humanism, this *measurement* of consciousness, I propose, must also be an objective *phenomenal measure* of what is central to the human spirit!

All three of the axioms of anthropomorphic optics are operating all of the time in everyday life. This special power of consciousness must always be a potent factor in how we perceive the qualities in the world. The two—the physical through the stereoscopic presentation, and the "mental"—were pitted against one another to provide a measure here of the amount of the effect of the "mental" upon the physical. That so-called "mental" effect is the actual effect of *consciousness*. I suggest that that measure of consciousness, especially, must also be a measure of something along the lines of what I have been calling *spirit* upon all of our human experiences.

Like appurtenance, symbolizing all by itself, has been shown to affect our awareness of the color of an object: when a neutral colored outline of a tomato is symbolized as a tomato, it is perceived as redder than when its outline is not tomato-like. In a like fashion a lemon outline referred to by the experimenter as a lemon is perceived as yellower than its neutral colored outline. In another experiment it was found that when one merely imagines one of the parts of a geometrical illusion, the illusory effect is at least as great as the actual physical illusion itself is. Imagination, I suggest, arises out of the fact that we symbolize events to ourselves. The *images* upon which human *imagination* is based are re-presentations of events to ourselves. Then they may become idealized in our awareness. At least seven confirmations of this axiom, and for each of the other two axioms, exist in the literature.

These three axioms, I am proposing, comprise the three components that make up what I am calling our spiritual human natures. These effects on what appear to us as awarenesses of things and happenings, and as events in our consciousness go far beyond anything physical. Just as has been the case with cortical expressivity, it is also true that appurtenance and our symbolizing propensities, which are so evident in our daily lives, can be brought into laboratory settings. In this way they operate in ways analogous to the physicists' vacuum. And then altogether they show us something of what I am calling the evidence of the spirit in humanity.

These examples of the effects of symbolizing on human experiencing along with the those of appurtenance and the expressivity of our cortices, are all factual evidence for the presence of something of the spirit in human existence. When the theoretical proposals are brought into a laboratory setting they demonstrate the comparability of these data to the physicists' introduction of the vacuum to prove he can explain the fall of a leaf from the tree. Though this theory has not been mathematized, its components otherwise are able to predict laboratory phenomena accurately. As a result the theory can be accorded the same kind of provisional acceptance that we grant to physics. Because we give credence to physics in relation to falling leaves, these factors of expressivity, appurtenance and symbolizing can also be given some credence as the basis for the more complex phenomena that we see, hear, feel and experience generally in everyday life according to this anthropomorphic theory of perception.

But more important than the theory even are the data that these experiments have disclosed. These laboratory phenomena all indicate that what people see under such conditions are not equal to what would have been predicted on the basis of the physiological stimulation that is impressed on the retina by the external physical stimulation. It has been assumed by common sense and physiology that we see what is physically-physiologically there in the world—except for the geometrical illusions which are thought of as errors of perception. But these so-called geometrical illusions, research has shown, are seen by everyone all over the world. If they are, indeed, *illusory*, then all of our human experiences of our visual worlds must all be *illusory*. And, of course, we do not so construe them, for they are not. We see on the basis of what our enspirited brain does to the incoming physical-physiological stimulation. The results of the experiments indicate the individual nature of the percepts of everyone, simply because every human brain is individual.

These data all indicate that we do not see what is simply there on the basis of physiology and physics, not exactly. Instead, we see according to the ways human beings see, and that is according to our individual psychological awarenesses. As my teacher Heinz Werner indicated in the *Journal de Psychologie* as early as 1934 in discussing the geometrical illusions, "In other words, those facts which first appear to be exceptions . . . are not illusions, but phenomena which illuminate the general structure of perception in a . . . striking . . . way." The laboratory data that I have reported above all "illuminate the general structure" of the contents of our awarenesses, for perception, as I have said, is just a term for awareness. In the last couple of decades much research has shown, as I reported above, that the awareness of any of the geometrical illusion's so-called illusory characters are easily destroyed merely by separating their parts stereoscopically. How the parts pertain to one another determines whether an illusory effect will occur: When the parts pertain by being at the same depth, the illusion occurs; when the parts are separated in space, the illusion disappears. Furthermore, the generalized theory predicts that we see in such ways rather than as the old set of physiological-physical assumptions would have it—as equaling the physical-physiological stimulation. These data also, however, indicate that seeing is individual, but close enough grossly to what we can agree upon in everyday life, so that we can get along with one another.

This anthropomorphic theory of perception suggests that it is according to the components of expressivity, appurtenance, and their symbolization that these awarenesses have occurred. Of course, what we see is always in conjunction with what is also there neurologically, physiologically, and physically, but we each see an entirely individual world—enspirited by something, something beyond the physical and the physiological. The three theoretical psychological components that I set forth, I am suggesting as the basis of that enspiriting. Of course, theories are 'always,' as Einstein suggested, 'subject to question and doubt.' That the theory will surely in time prove to have been at least incomplete, is to be expected. What is important are the data which show the discrepancies between the incoming stimulation and the enspirited awarenesses. That is where our sense experiences have to differ from the instrumental findings of physics. The differences between our and their results are what are important. It is the data which show that even in our sensory awarenesses of our worlds, even in those awarenesses not tested, those arising from touch and taste and the other sense organs too, they are all, I suggest, experiencings to which we bring something, something that I am calling spirited, to our awarenesses. It is these awarenesses which have been transformed by some psychological-neural process, this theoretical one or some other, which allows for the extremes in individuality that arise in human consciousness and in creativity, and is lacking in the instrumental findings of physics.

These three proposals and their data comprise a current scientific psychological theory applied only and specifically to humans from which our awarenesses and our consciousness result. The components of consciousness, I suggest, are based also upon our cortical expressivity, appurtenance and our symbolic ways of representing human experiences. The experience of consciousness that arises from registrations and awarenesses are also a function of these three factors. But in consciousness we move a step beyond awarenesses themselves. Our awarenesses of consciousness, and especially our awarenesses in our reflective consciousnesses, are also what much more sharply than awarenesses comprise the spirit that is the basis for spiritual humanism.

There may be other factors involved that I have not considered. Or mine may even be the wrong ones, and the theory may be dead wrong, but the data are not wrong. These theoretical components, it seems to me, can provide temporarily, at least, to some extent as a minimum, some of the basic qualities that one can find in a definition of a human spirit. The sense in us of something beyond merely bodily experience resides in the awarenesses that are accounted for by the theory. Then beyond these sensory awarenesses there is the non sensory awareness of consciousness itself. It is from this consciousness that we may have a sense of at least a partial other to whom we talk to within ourselves. For some the experience may be so definite that another being seems to be occupying their skin. But we have all had some such experience of what arises from consciousness that in children can be epitomized in the phrase, 'Me, myself, and I,' three views of the self: as object, as being, and as subject. These awarenesses arise from natural sources in our human natures—I trust from natural sources something like those that I have outlined here in this anthropomorphic scientific theory of human experience. Spiritual humanism is founded on the human psychological processes of awareness and consciousness of which the theory tries to give an account.

One further point is important here, especially at the dawn of the power of DNA. DNA may directly effect the level of cortical expressivity, and perhaps even continue to do so as we pass from infancy to adolescence and beyond. But the DNA can have no *direct* effect upon *our feeling values*, nor upon our *thoughts and consciousness*. These latter two depend upon the further transformation of our experiences by "reentrant circuits" and the actions of our symbolizing frontal lobes. The cumulative effects of our daily human experiencings on the brain would overcome any effects that the level of DNA would have on them. Such DNA effects, if any, would have to be indirect in the extreme. The inherited DNA would have to be routed through those complex brain processes, and the conclusions drawn from the accumulation of all of our daily experiencings. DNA would have to be limited to direct effects upon cortical expressivity only, for there is no precise localization for our thoughts, consciousness and values as there is for cortical expressivity.

Please note that I have not yet tried to give an explanation of why we act as we do. That larger task requires that the roles of thinking and feeling extend beyond the components outlined.

CHAPTER V

Thinking, Artificial Intelligence, and Why People Act as They Do

In the late 1960s some of the seniors at Bennington College felt that they had a new challenge to face: The Vietnam War had brought about great changes in the young men of that era, and the young women had also been deeply affected. A new and more complex component had apparently entered into their lives. Previously it had largely been a matter of accepting a job offer, getting married, or going to graduate school. But suddenly the lives of these young women had been somehow disrupted and in a way enlarged. One of them told it to me very well. She was not concerned with those old issues, she said, but with what sort of *life style* should she consider for herself. Where should she live to carry out that life style. Living with someone rather than marriage had become an option. New decisions brought on by all of the disruptions in the course and tenor the lives of so many of the young men were affecting the young women of that generation too. The effects were different for their men friends, of course, but the disruption and disaffection affected the women too. There was no current man in her life, so that was not an immediate concern, but she did not want to set up a life that would preclude that as a future possibility. I saw the chance that I had been looking for for two decades—to study real human thinking about real human problems.

Instead of the artificial laboratory situations that had been used in the past, I saw that this new development in their lives was an opportunity to study thinking under truly real life circumstances. As I said the traditional issues for seniors had been: Do I go to graduate school? Do I take the job that has been offered to me? Do I get married? Sometimes the questions were met singlely and sometimes all or a couple of them at once. But the climate of living had changed during those Vietnam war years, at least for some of them, and the questions had become much more generally: What kind of life style is right for me? Where shall I live—geographically, that is—to foster that life style? Do I set up housekeeping with the guy I've been seeing? I had all along been finding a much more thoughtful group of people among these more alienated young persons than in previous generations of students. So the questions they posed for themselves reflected those changes: What kind of life do I want to live given who I am and the skills I have acquired—do I know who I am? I think I know my skills. What kind of life am I prepared now to live knowing that? How do I find out more about myself? Where am I likely to find my friends living, and where will I have the opportunity to make new ones? These very real issues called for serious thought about the decisions they would soon have to make.

Clearly they wanted to think things out and I wanted to study the thinking that could go on as they would speak their concerns aloud. I had failed to develop a way of studying language and thought in graduate school two decades previously, though I had been supported for a year to do just that. I was then shunted onto the study of visual perception, but I never let my first love—thinking and language—stray far from my concerns. So I decided to offer to seniors the opportunity to examine their real issues, and any others of a broadly educational content—so long as I could study the relations of thinking and language. I insisted that they fulfill three requirements I placed upon them: They had to fill out a questionaire (that would allow me briefly to assess whether they really needed psychotherapy rather than what I was offering them); They had to allow the Educational Interchanges—as I called them—to be recorded, so I could study the thinking process; And they had to be willing that I use the materials, even quoting from them directly, if I published the findings. Thirty-three seniors fulfilled these requirements, and wished to explore these broad educational questions during the college years 1970 and 1971.

I used a modified procedure pioneered by Carl Rogers. I listened to each statement they expressed, and tried to understand exactly what they had said. I tested my understanding by stating back in my own words what I understood them to say. I found I was in general quite good at it, because I received very few corrections—but those I received helped me to understand what I was missing. (Perhaps I should add here that I had spent the last three years obtaining the credentials to be licensed as a psychotherapist, and obtained my license in 1971.) I did not, as Carl Rogers had done, emphasize feelings, but I did find that thought and feeling were always—so it seemed to me—inextricably intertwined. I was able to find a general pattern. That was: How, actually and concretely, to live their lives, and what might be the obstacles or problems in the way of doing that, given the nature of who they had become over these last several years? Since Bennington College fostered the education of each individual student so that she (it was then a women's college) could fulfill her interests and skills, both in the courses she took and in the work she did during four Non Resident Terms, many of them seemed to know themselves in these regards rather well. As persons, of course, there was much more yet to be known, but they could hardly be aware of that for that would require the years after they graduated to let them know about those further issues of living.

There was, furthermore, a pattern as to how their thinking went. On the first meeting they usually set out all, or most, of the problematical aspects of their life issues as they saw them: style of life as opposed to family expectations, their own hopes and fears, and sometimes dreams, and the difficulties they faced among the expectations of their families, friends or lovers, and the life they wanted given what they had accomplished and who they were. Some were not sure they knew that latter. Many simply were not willing to accept the traditional role expectations that had been placed upon women for many years. Those issues usually took one or two forty-five minute sessions two weeks apart to set out the problems or issues as they saw them. Then there would be a meeting, or perhaps two, where problems and obstacles would all be confused with ideas and hopes for a solution. And then I would be presented with a kind of solution, perhaps a rather tenuous one in the next meeting, but sometimes a very definite one—and they were gone. Usually at that point they saw the old problems in a new way, or they had a sense that it was all right, that things would work out, or, yes, now I know what I will do—often with great certainty. One wonderful example I must tell. She came in and set out very clearly the situation and the difficulties that she saw in the first meeting. She ended by saying, "So you see, it's really impossible!" Two weeks later she returned in a great rush, and said, "Turn on the machine. I want to tell you this. What I learned here was that I always have problems! And I always solve my problems! I have no time for this. Thank you very much!" That was not, however, typical.

An illustration will show how thinking proceeded as a serious human being thought, even though it too was not really typical. This senior was a person I had never had contact with, and this was now the Spring term—her last before graduation. She was in a very tense state when she appeared, but she was apparently reassured by the way I listened and merely tried to understand or become clear on what she meant. I found out shortly that she also knew well a student who had worked closely with me. Her problem will not seem very important or a crucial one on the surface, but it was. And it was especially problematical to her as seen from her perspective. The young man with whom she was in love had asked her to marry him. What was the problem? He was a wonderful guy. The other night when she had talked to him on the telephone she had been a little upset about one of her courses. When she finished talking she felt better and thought no more about it. When she woke up in the morning she found him asleep in his sleeping bag on the floor beside her bed. She was astonished. "What are you doing here?" She was shocked, though also pleased to see him, and chagrined that her upset had led him to have driven some hours from Yale, or was it Wesleyan, to get there. He merely said that she had been upset, so he had come to be with her.

She had not had that kind of upset, but how could she not love such a guy. Furthermore, he came from a good family, and it was one that her family found comparable to and compatable with theirs. They had met briefly and liked one another. And her family really liked him. They hoped that they would marry. Though her family had not wanted her to go to Bennington College, nor had they approved really of her choice of courses or her major, they did now express their approval. So what was the problem?

    She never really told me in so many words what the problem was, but she had gone to the college of her choice despite the fact that her family had wanted her to go elsewhere. She went because her family was too good, and they had all along had a too powerful an effect upon her life. She could not find herself among them; she had to get away on her own. Their pressure on her course choices through the college years was not oppressive, but it was something she had constantly in awareness. She had insisted in going her own way, and had gone her own way. And she had been successful. And now they approved; they were not grudging; she knew that they really were fine people. But! Her problem came out as "How can I do this conventional thing?" Get married when I graduate as all of the conventional young college women do? But the problem was much deeper than that. It was more like: Have I really established myself as my own being? Am I strong enough in myself not to become another's person rather than my own person? Have I really achieved my independence, and can I depend upon having achieved it with this wonderful, but strong person who knows himself very well, so that I don't succumb to giving over myself as I had almost done with my family? And as I had seen my mother do before me? These were real life questions that brought forth her deepest thought. It was her deepest thought, but brought on by her deepest feelings, and all of her thought was thoroughly embroiled with feelings and emotions.

    It was these latter issues that formed the contents of seven Educational Interchanges. She solved her problem, for in the course of the Interchanges she realized over time that she really did feel that she knew now who she was. In the examination of what was in her awareness and consciousness she began to trust in the solidity of the person she was, since she had had the time to contemplate herself now in some depth, who she, herself, was now. This example does not sound to me like a problem in chess that AI is so fine at solving.

It is not a problem that AI (strong or weak) will ever solve, first, because they have to begin with objective data. That is all they have. They do not begin with the awarenesses that are individual and different from what is presented through physiological-physical means. They know nothing about these awarenesses that have been studied by experimenters in visual perception. Their assumptions go right past that absolutely necessary step. Then they have no concerns for feelings, or if you wish, feeling laden thoughts that we human beings have as the basis for our thinking. And, of course, though those feelings are behind the motivational thrust that powers our thinking, the AI investigators have no motivational thrust arising from such personal powerful needs. Furthermore, this senior's real problem begins in the personal awarenesses and full consciousness that only she had. No one else presented this problem. And recall as well that these are her individual awarenesses that make up an individual consciousness that the AI investigators are totally unable to replicate. These are not the givens that AI deals with; what is provided there is the same for all, as are all of the problems of AI. Her very sensory awarenesses were those she carried with her throughout her growth and upbringing. They had in time become awarenesses as memories in her consciousness. These emerged as we talked, and there I encountered the complex consciousness that was hers and hers alone. The adherents of AI presume that those awarenesses do not exist, for they certainly do not exist for their computers. They also assume that whatever substitutes there for our awarenesses would not be individual, but would be common to all. They are not.

Then, if they consider consciousness, which I believe they do not, it too would be the same for all who approach the machine. My senior student's consciousness was hers and hers alone; no one else had her problem, and no one else will ever have precisely her problem. Furthermore, it was an agonizing problem; it was emotionally terribly upsetting to her, and quite reasonably so. At times she cried in the uncertainty of being clearly certain of who she was and to what extent her sense of herself was strong enough to withstand the power of another person upon her. That can be a terribly difficult question for women, for if she and her lover are to have children, then she is necssarily going to be in an extremely dependent position for a period of time. And then there is the effect of the dependence of a child upon one's determination to be one's own person. These are not abstract problems to be solved by a computer. These are powerful issues that form the essential basis of our living. And living is not simply an abstract and objective problem to be solved. These issues are a matter of the life and death of the spirit. The SAI adherents, and even Penrose's more balanced focus upon consciousness, have the issues of life all awry. It is human values which are at issue here—central human feeling values. It is her values; it is what mattered to this young woman, what mattered to the very depths of her being that were involved. Was she now who she had been trying to become? Could she depend upon her feelings to know what mattered to know for certain that she had achieved her maturity so strongly that it could withstand the powers of her lover and the will of her family? This was her problem.

Consciousness, through the Educational Interchanges, was to become part of her salvation, but it was her selfhood for herself that mattered. It was a value situation that is ignored by AI adherents, and by all those who are totally focussed on cognition over the broader issues of human values that arise out of our feelings. I am speaking of feelings, not as emotionality, but as those indicators of what matter most deeply to the person. The hypothalamus and the limbic system have long been known as involving the emotions, but in human beings the outcomes of our total thalamo-cortical-limbic complex are our feelings, our feelings of the values of things. For given the nature of our thalamo-cortical-limbic sytsems those impulses pass through the frontal lobes, and add reflective processes to what would be emotions and turn them into feelings of value. C. G. Jung has suggested that feeling is as rational a function as thinking, because in both reflection can be brought to bear upon what otherwise might only be emotion.

In animals the latter is probably all that is possible, but with our frontal lobes operating on our hypothalamus and limbic systems a different outcome has become possible. Possible, I say, not certain, of course, because whether and how we reflect will depend upon whether we are driven by emotions or by feelings of what matters most in our lives. The SAI adherents have no hypothalamus or limbic systems in their machines—and they appear to forget that they have them in their own nervous systems. Their machines will never match actual human thought.

The AI machines at least will never match human thought until they have developed ones that can duplicate our thalamo-cortical-limbic systems. I wish them luck, but I think that they need to reassess just what it is that they face. They need to study human thought, before they conclude that their computers can achieve it. They also need to study human awarenesses. What the senior did was to assess who she had become in the midst of not really having had time to think about those matters previously. These concerns were broadly educational in scope, even though they were not part of a subject matter course. She found from examining what she had done, the decisions about her courses that she had made all along, the successful work terms, and the successful outcomes that she had achieved both there and in the other areas of her college life—the more personal ones—that perhaps, just perhaps at first, that maybe she was pretty much her own being. During our sometimes tearful interchanges, there began to emerge a sense of herself which through all of this time and by all of her own efforts she had become. She was constantly assessing what mattered to her, what she felt, and over a period of some months of meetings she gained a sense of who she had become. So it was in time that she was able to conclude finally, that whatever decision she made would be hers and not his, nor perhaps most important, not ever theirs—her family's. This result plainly required the agonizing thought I've described, for what she was contemplating doing was indistinguishable objectively from giving in to her family's wishes—marrying the man she loved and of whom they approved in the summer after her graduation from college. She did act in accordance with the conclusions she had reached.

How would AI handle that delemma? Would it be a delemma for a computer? She had to make an internal distinction between what was conventional and what she was going to do, and the distinction was impossible to distinguish, except from her perspective. The decision also had to satisfy her, and be one that she could trust herself to be able to act upon. Is there a place for such trust in a computer? No algorithm would do here; this was no chess game. This problem was a matter of her very life's worth, whether she could live her life or succumb to the life of another. Of course, her consciousness was intimately related to every awareness she had and that she considered.

Real thinking, real life thinking is never apart from the living parts of life that matter to us as much as life itself does, for it is life itself that is there involved. Life, or a living death brought on by what we only thought were our own decisions, can be the outcome without deep thinking and a full consciousness. Real thought is beyond the logic of an algorithm. The people who make decisions on the stock market using their own money are not dealing in algorithms—though the institutional managers of stocks may well be doing just that. But then they are not thinking, but merely applying a set rule, an algorithm. The rule may be based upon logic, but life decisions arise out of feeling, powerful feelings of value that are personal and arise within a person. Pure logic is seldom at issue in thinking about the matters of life.

Indeed, pure logic is not involved in thinking one's way through to a theory in physics. That at least is true even for the theoretical physicist, Albert Einstein, as he shows us by the nonlogical nature of his thinking. I use Einstein's own words as he describes his awarenesses, consciousness and thought to show that his thought, too, even though it is about a theory in physics, is thought that is powered by feeling rather than by the dessicated quality of an algorithm. His thinking too shows the fraught kind of feeling about what matters that characterized the young woman's thinking. What Einstein was aware of as he spent seven long years until he created the special theory of relativity demonstrate that he was not dealing with an algorithm.

Einstein was only sixteen when he first became aware of the problems of physics, but it was not until he was eighteen or nineteen that he became entirely engrossed in them. Then he spent seven long years—until he published the special theory of relativity in 1905—at times almost despairing, as he sought the solution to his self-imposed problem. He too was powerfully motivated by feelings that led him to assay a solution to the problems of a general physical theory. The three components I outlined in the previous chapter are intended to comprise a psychological theory from which even the consciousness required by thinking creative thoughts can result. An examination of Einstein's processes as he worked on the special theory of relativity can serve as a kind of informal test of the theory's ability to deal with creative thought, though I frankly believe that the young woman's thought was also creative.

Einstein was interviewed by the psychologist Max Wertheimer about his recollections of his thought processes while he was trying to create what turned out to be the special theory of relativity. Einstein reported to Wertheimer in *Productive Thinking*: "I very rarely think in words at all." And then he went on to say:

> During all those years there was a feeling of direction, of going straight toward something concrete. . . . Of course, behind such a direction there is always something logical; but I have it in a kind of survey, in a way visually.

Einstein's thinking appears to be in the form of some kind of visual imagery, marked by feeling that he was moving in the right direction. But as he noted, there was no lack of logic to what he was thinking, though it certainly was very far from an algorithm. It was not logical thinking in the usual sense of that term; it was very idiosyncratic thinking, indeed, and was full of images rather than words. As he had indicated, he rarely thought in words.

In his *Autobiographical Notes* he was clearer about the nature of his visual imagery:

> The psychical entities which seem to serve as elements of thought are certain signs and more or less clear images which can be 'voluntarily' reproduced and combined. . . . The above mentioned elements are, in my case, of visual and some muscular type. Conventional words . . . have to be searched for laboriously only in a second stage. . . .

Wordless visual and muscular images are the basis for the combinations he played with over the seven long years, during which he sometimes felt despair. Penrose also used the above quotation to show that images rather than words are the components of even the highest level of mathematical thought. That was in part the basis for his conclusion that SAI could not really account for thought. I agree with his evaluation. However, he does not stress the powerful feelings that led to those long years of thought that Einstein also reports. It is because Penrose is not a psychologist who is concerned with human actions, I believe, that he misplaces the meaning of consciousness from its ancillary role as necessary for thinking, to a central role. It is thinking in the realm of consciousness through which Einstein proceeded, but the thinking proceeded from his powerful feeling that such a theory was of the greatest importance. Of course, some of his thoughts that became clear in time were not clear at the beginning of his quest.

The issues in physics mattered so deeply to Einstein that they precluded essentially all other interests. He thought about them constantly, and examined the issues often along with speculations about what might happen under impossible circumstances, for example, riding on a beam of light. His speculations took place in consciousness; he entertained such speculations in full awareness over and over again. These were, of course, not the idle speculations that all of us entertain, but were consciously entertained thoughts which helped him finally to rethink the crucial issues. Just how one could determine whether two events were indeed simultaneous had been left to common sense, but Einstein came to realize that the measured determination of simultaneity was central to the new physics that he was formulating. He says in this regard in the *Notes*:

> Today everyone knows, of course, that all attempts to clarify this . . . satisfactorily were condemned to failure as long as the axiom of the absolute character of time, viz., simultaneity, unrecognizedly was anchored in the unconscious.

By that he meant that the concept of simultaneity had not been thought through theoretically so that its vague and theoretically useless common sense meaning could be extricated for theoretical use.

So he also speculated on what would happen to him on his beam of light in relation to someone riding on another beam of light. The reformulation of the issue of simultaneity was one of the crucial factors in overcoming the Newtonian theory. So his thought consisted of these rather vague visual images, of a kind of directional sort, which implied to him that he was moving forward. But integral to all of this thinking was the drive that led him to think, and think hard for seven long years. The three components of the psychological theory—expressivity, appurtenance, symbolizing—these are, I, at least, believe are all also components operating during his quest.

Einstein's imagination arose from the kind of symbolizing that he engaged in; his seven year-long quest arose from what pertained to him so deeply; and his expressivity is evident as basic to both of the others throughout that whole long trying period. The components of the theory are not so neatly separated in his creative thinking of course. The expressivity is also in the imagination that symbolically came to him in images of direction; the symbolization is in the imaged thought of riding on beams of light through which he meant to solve the problem that mattered so much to him, pertained so powerfully to him—and to him alone. Einstein's creativity arose also out of what he registered, what he was aware of, and what was in his consciousness—and especially what he reflected upon within his consciousness. The theory was composed out of the expressivity that was so evident in his thought, the overpowering value to him of his quest—nothing else seems to have mattered to him—and the free symbolizing of his imagination. These three factors which account for the experiences of observers in laboratory settings appear to be appropriate also in providing a reasonable, though after-the-fact interpretation of the creativity of an Einstein. It was out of his psychological experiences documented here, I suggest, that the Special Theory of Relativity appears to have arisen.

Why did Einstein act as he did, then? The answer provided by the theory in general terms is that he felt that a new physical theory of the universe was so important, he valued such a theory so highly that he persevered for seven long years in his effort to devise it. He struggled mightily on, pressed by his feelings for a mere idea (a spiritual quest?); that value laden quest sometimes left him almost despairing. He reflected upon his rather vague visual images, awarenesses in thought, of conflicting movements of observers, his feelings of directedness, his imaged motions of light, his imaginary rides on light beams, and the precise physical facts that he knew so well. He was driven all along by the spirit of his dream of a unified theory of physics—more a desire than a thought. What shall we call such feeling laden thoughts? Then he persevered by further imagining outlandish physical motions (riding on one beam of light in relation to someone riding on another) with his knowledge of Newtonian theory and the physical facts always in the background. At one point he asked himself, "What *is* the speed of light?" which, of course, he very well knew, but he had not then grasped its new significance in what was to become his new theory. Out of these reflections in consciousness he ultimately came to an abstract mathematical conclusion about how to reconceive the theoretical propositions that would fulfill his task. This conclusion involved, just as had Galileo's before him, events that could not occur physically.

Galileo had concluded the operation of inertia that could never happen on the earth, and thereby set physical theory on its modern path. Einstein concluded his mathematical outcomes, finally, because they allowed him to predict events that were correct and extended beyond the boundaries that Newton's theory had envisioned. His formulae were not factual; they even lead to physical absurdities. But the abstract formulae allowed him to predict events in near and in outer space better than the Newtonian formulae. He conducted himself as he did, because he had envisioned a symbolic formula of an entirely abstracted kind that could encompass facts heretofore unencompassable by any physical theory. It clearly was for him the most important event in his awarenesses of his life—the life on which he had expended seven long years to accomplish. Theorizing was his highest value and had been the basis of his thought and actions for seven long years. Einstein acted as he did because his awarenesses arising from his expressive nature led him to symbolize the construction of a general physical theory as the most important value in life. That was why he spent the major portion of his life as he did. That is why Einstein acted as he did.

It is the case then that Einstein's physical theory arose from his psychological processes, perhaps even as they have been outlined above. Physics arose before psychology as a discipline, because it involved simpler materials and phenomena upon which its theories could first be devised and tested. Newton's theory ignored everything but the relations between physical objects to account for their motions. The moon and the earth, the apple and the earth, any two bodies were related according to two kinds of motion: inertial and gravitational. So too then is the relation of the leaf to the earth—except for the factors which cannot be controlled. But the actions of human beings on the earth could not explained by those factors—except in free fall, and even those do not explain the frantic movements, and the scream that issues from the throat. The actions of human beings on earth are a function of the components of human awarenesses and consciousness: I suggest that these components are expressivity, appurtenance, and symbolizing. The creativity displayed by physicists has to be accounted for by psychological principles, not physical ones. I don't expect mine to be the last such attempt, but it has some things to recommend it as these two chapters have tried to show.

Consciousness clearly plays a large role in human thinking and even in creative thought. But what is central to the enterprise of thinking within consciousness is the feeling that impels us to solve what troubles us and, perhaps, puzzles us. John Dewey long ago, suggested that reflective thought, that is thoughts and ideas entertained in consciousness, arose when one felt a problem. There may be other occasions for thought, but the human examples set forth here do, indeed, confirm that view. The thoughts themselves may at first be vague images, as the notion of simultaneity was for Einstein, but the process of thinking has a directedness that is precise. It moves inexorably toward its goal. In these examples the goal was clarification. But in the former example it was clarification for maintaining her selfhood for herself, while in the latter it was clarification for the purpose of a grand theory.

Why did the young woman act as she did, that is, decide to marry immediately upon graduating from college? She made that decision because she could now trust her reasons for doing that no matter how conventional her decision might look to an outsider.

Why did Einstein act as he did? Einstein sought that theory of physics that would unite what had become disparate, because he felt that it was the most important thing in the world to do.

They both acted as they did on the basis of what mattered to them once they had clarified the central issues in their lives. Why people act as they do is based upon how they feel about the events they have symbolized on the basis of their given level of cortical expressivity.

CHAPTER VI

Psychologizing Physics

In *Optics: The Science of Vision* Vasco Ronchi reveals how physicists, though never saying that they were doing that, removed the study of optics from our human eyes and vision, to instruments which did not have the individual qualities that human eyes and seeing display. The study of optics goes back more than two thousand years, and, originally, as Ronchi says, "It was an *anthropmorphic physics,* a science in which the chief figure was sentient man." They were seeking to determine how people came to know the external world through the senses. Their conclusions may be of interest to those who have read Chapter IV above, especially since it seemingly allies me with the ancients rather than the moderns. Ronchi reports that the ancients:

> soon reached the conclusion that senses existed, which functioned through peripheral organs. These were linked by nerves to a central organ, the brain, where dwelt the soul or mind. . . . These signals, having been received and analyzed by the mind are represented in specific ways. Thus those arriving along the nerves connected . . . to the eyes are *represented* by light and color.
>
> At that time there was a general conviction that . . . light and color . . . were *psychical representations,* entities created by the mind in order to represent the signals reaching it from the external world. . . .

All I find to disagree with in the view of the ancients is that it is the brain that does that analyzing, rather than the mind. (Note that it is the mind and not the soul that does the analyzing!) Indeed, it is the consciousness arising from my brain, which formulated the axioms of the theory of anthropomorphic optics, that has done the analyzing and the synthesizing.

I substitute for the commonsensical mind the symbolizing component of my theorizing, and for the commonsensical soul, I substitute the appurtenant values that we human beings develop during our lifetimes. These latter distinctions appear to be in accordance with current usage, for the dictionary, when it makes a distinction between soul and mind, indicates that the former has more to do with values and conscience, and the latter with cognition and knowledge. The soul does not analyze; it has the moral function of determining right from wrong. But those two, especially, appurtenance and symbolizing, along with cortical expressivity, I suggest, are the components which take the place of the ancients' soul, and the common sense soul and mind, and what I call spirit. Furthermore, I would say that what we are visually aware of is a psychological presentation, rather than a re-presentation. Our individual psychological makeups, in conjunction with the physical and physiological, and then the neurological contribution of the brain, cause the awarenesses we experience to arise as presences in us. In a sense Ronchi's statement that "The mind's capacity to create . . . lights and colors . . ." is true (not the soul's note), but only a partial truth because it overlooks the necessary factors of the physical and physiological inputs. And it is the theoretical components that I outlined in Chapter IV, and not mind, that are the sufficient conditions to create the qualities of the colors in the light that we see.

In Ronchi's view a solution arose when the light that we see—*lux* in Latin—became *lumen*—what physicists measured through objects, actually through their instruments. As was true in the astronomer's measurement of the transit of a star, physicists long ago removed the human factor from their measurements by exclusively using instrumental devices through which they measured their phenomena. There are, accordingly, consequences to starting with psychological events rather than the instrumentally measured ones of physics, perhaps even for physics itself. Please notice what the physicists back there did without telling anyone: They substituted for *lux*, the light we all, including physicists, actually see, for a *lumen*, which no one ever sees, because it can only be apprehended by their physical devices, by instruments—not human eyes. Furthermore, as Ronchi says:

> Even though the philosophers of the later Middle Ages had many profound differences . . . none of them opposed this lucid and exhaustive position, which held the subjective *lux* to be the effect of the objective *lumen*.
>
> It had also been made quite evident . . . that everything which was seen, precisely because it was a mass of figures created by the mind of each observer, was highly personal and subjective in character.

Absolutely so, absolutely "personal"—except that the *lux* or light that we do see is an effect of the externally presented *lumen* or instrumentally measured photons nowadays in conjunction with our individual physiological and psychological components.

Everything seen is, indeed, personal and idiosycratic, and in current terminology, since the 1800s "subjective," but phenomenally real as all of the data of Chapter IV demonstrate. But when Ronchi continues, I have a problem, for he says,

> Ancient optics, then, was definitely not objective and not physical, in the modern sense of the word, but had a purely subjective phenomenon as its foundation.

And it is important that Ronchi added in relation to the word "objective," the additional words "in the modern sense of the word," for the ancient sense of the word "objective" had our current meaning of the word "subjective." According to the *The Oxford English Dictionary* the word "subjective" in the seventeenth century was defined as "pertaining to the essence or reality of a thing; real, essential." At that same time the word "objective" meant "existing as an object of consciousness, as distinct from having any real existence." "Subjective" meant "real," and "objective" meant nonexistent or existing only "as an object of consciousness." In the beginning of the 1700s "subjective" began to lose its then objective character, and "objective" became more and more ascendant. Subjective came to mean in time "existing in the mind only." So that now objectivity is prized as a real reality and subjectivity is belittled as unreal.

Poor Goethe, great poet though he was, when he challanged the great physicist Newton's color theory, he was vilified, laughed at, and degraded. But the differences between the so-called objective Newton, who held the prism at arms length and at right angles to the light, so that the refracted light could be seen on the wall to his left, and the phenomenologist Goethe, who looked directly at the prism with the refracted light shining through into his eyes, were real. With the reversal of the meaning of the terms "subjective" and "objective," however, Newton now became objective and Goethe merely subjective! Goethe's phenomenological awareness, though it had formerly been *objective*, had no power against the new definition of objectivity which fostered Newton and his views. Though a few decades earlier they would have been subjective and objective, respectively in the reverse, Newton triumphed. I followed Goethe in Chapter IV. But there was one significant addition that was not true for Goethe: the data I referred to had all been measured by objects; Goethe's phenomenological observations became objectively measured phenomen*al* awarenesses; thus they are just as objective as all of the instrumental measures of physicists, since all were measured by objects.

The great difference between the psychological measures and those of the physicists, however, is that the experimental data I referred to were all obtained by using objects to measure the awarenesses of human beings rather than using instruments to measure physical light by eliminating any individual person's awarenesses. Just as physics gains objectivity by using instruments of measurement, so too does psychology become objective by using objects to obtain their measures.

In both cases, of course, we are only relatively objective, because all of the measures arise in the end with some subjective human being using objects to make the measurement. The words "subjective" and "objective" create unnecessary problems as their histories demonstrate. The results of psychological experiments do not at all match the accuracy that instrumentally based physical experiments achieve, but neither is more objective—or less subjective. All human enterprises, in these terms, are subjective ultimately.

What took place in the seventeenth century has been called a scientific revolution. Actually, it was a physics and astronomy revolution. Psychology became thought of as a purely subjective enterprise. The most important aspect of human experience, how we and the world meet in our human awarenesses, became "subjective," and to minds not as great as Goethe's, psychology became an ephemeral enterprise ever since. In 1959 an article was published in a psychologial journal which brought forth Goethe's real phenomenological meaning, so that it could really be appreciated. A follow-up article was mentioned as an expansion of the position, but when I enquired of the writer where the second article had been published, he replied that he had not been able to publish it. Prejudices toward the non physical, the phenomenal, even when objectively measured still run deep.

Back in the 1920s a new view of scientific definitions arose which was largely based on the consequences of Einstein's theory of relativity. Henceforth a definition of a concept would not be considered to be scientific unless the physical operations were available to demonstrate its factuality. This prescription arose directly from Einstein's reformulation of the concept of simultaneity. Two events separated in space could not be called simultaneous any longer unless physicists had the means to determine through measurements that the two events were, indeed, simultaneous. The common sense and Newtonian views of simultaneity had become obsolete and useless with the new physics that Einstein had inaugurated. A whole book was written delineating the meaning and the consequences of this new development. One of the consequences of this definition requiring measured operations, along with the new developments in physical knowledge, was that the operations used to measure a physical event had to be included as a part of that result. The observational devices had to be taken into consideration in determining the outcomes. One of the outcomes has resulted in their awareness that what they call "indeterminacy" has become part of their problem. The location and the speed of an object could no longer be determined at one and the same time: One could gauge the speed, or one could measure the location, but not both speed and location by the same measuring device at the same time.

In the psychological experiments reported in Chapter IV the three explanatory concepts of cortical expressivity, appurtenance, and symbolization were also defined operationally. In those instances groups of individual observers display awarenesses that in each case do not equal what would have been expected if the people did not bring something more to their awarenesses than the physical-physiological combinations would lead one to expect. That surplus, I believe, is a measure of at least one central component of the human spirit. Of course, there may be much more to the human spirit than what my three axioms suggest, but our awarenesses, composed of some set of processes such as those I have suggested, indicate a something beyond the physical-physiological that I am calling spirit. That spirit becomes more evident in consciousness, our reflection upon awarenesses, and in our reflective consciousnesses. As recently as 1982, however, a highly praised book by D. Marr entitled *Vision: A Computational Investigation into the Human Representation and Processing of Visual Information* took the view that such phenomena as I have referred to above merely show "by how wide a range of stimuli we can be fooled into saying that . . . differences exist where they objectively do not." Marr used the word "objectively" to mean that our phenomenal awarenesses are not the same as what one finds by employing objects to measure the physical phenomena presented to the observers. Moreover, he concludes that the responses of the observers are *wrong* in comparison to what the experimenter, of course, finds in measuring the stimuli with a ruler or other object. The actual differences between the observers' awarenesses and the experimenter's measures he discards evaluatively as "wrong." This prejudice against phenomenological observations, and even against *objectively measured phenomenal awarenesses* remains with us still.

And, of course, Marr and the many others who evaluate phenomena instead of examining it, would accordingly find no spirit at work as a result; he ruled out any quality of the human spirit by the assumption upon which he discards the findings as *unreal*, real data that he refuses to accept as evidence. But the evidences of the spirit are not mistakes that we make. Phenomenal evidence does not 'fool' us. They are true awarenesses that are always full of the human spirit.

The average human spirit, or some part of it at least, is attested to by the continual discrepancy between the physical-physiologial input and the measured psychological and phenomenal outcome. We do not see the world, whether we are observers in the laboratory or in everyday life, as it is given to us by our straightforward physical-physiological inputs. We bring something more which is, if you will, psychologically enspiriting. I am suggesting that that psychological enspiriting result could also be a measure of the spiritual nature that we find in the aspirations of humanity. I am not suggesting that there is no more than that to the human spirit, for I believe that there may be—but it may not yet have been measured, and it may even be immeasurable. But what has been measured in the experiments reported above attest to the reality of something beyond the physical-physiological and can be thought of as the human spirit that could be basic to spiritual humanism itself. The factors that define that spirit which I have set out, are, throughout, natural, not supernatural ones. The factors are theoretical and natural ones that have been bourne out by facts about ordinary people's awarenesses in measurable circumstances.

I have theorized that the ones I reported arise in the functioning of the cerebral cortex upon the systems of the hypothalamus and the limbic system which then affect our awarenesses of sensory events, and cause the enspiriting which is evidenced by their discrepancies with their physiological bases. I further theorize that there is a component of cortical expressivity that is present from birth onward. Appurtenance, I theorize, takes shape in the repeated encounters the infant has with her caretakers; she comes to value them and their ministrations; they become pertinent to her feeling of well being. Finally, I theorize that symbolic ways of representing these awarenesses, invaded by cortical expressivity and appurtenance, are present well before the first year is completed. I do not know that, but there are facts that lead me to that conclusion. These facts, I believe, indicate that at that time there are integrations of what had been largely separated and single awarenesses. The integrations may actually occur earlier, but I am being conservative in my estimate.

One fact that arises at about the end of the first year is that a child can pull something that he is holding in one hand out of it with the other hand—a physical integration. A second is that the child at that time often is able to walk; walking means that the unbalancing asymmetry required as one foot is put forth is integated with the other, and with a balancing act of the whole body. A third fact is that the average child speaks its first name at about that time—an integration of sight and articulated sound. And finally, the child is at ease in a strange place if either its father or its mother is present; it is as if the child grasped nonverbally, either one makes it all right—a very complex integration. But it is not at least until after a couple of years have passed, I believe, that a dawning awareness of awarenesses that I call consciousness arises. Once arisen consciousness goes through many stages. That consciousness shows major spurts in adolescence, though its potency then sometimes leads to severe self-consciousness, but that usually passes, and consciousness continues developing as it subsumes more awarenesses under its rubrics. As far as I can tell its development extends, and expands even, into and perhaps beyond old age. It is that same complex consciousness that is basic to the thinking that Einstein displayed. And it was that complex of thought powered by basic feelings that the young woman disclosed in working out through her own thought whether she had achieved the selfhood she required to be able to make the most important decision in her life.

The measures of the physicists are never affected by this undeniable human fact of individual awarenesses and consciousness.

That is the case, because they countered that possibility by using physical instruments that would preclude the individual human observations that would arise from their own unaided awarenesses. They deleted those "personal equations"—as they sometimes called them—from their measurements. They began that practice exclusively two centuries ago, because of the differing results in the transit of a star that they were obtaining from different observers. Indeed, the head of one institution fired his assistant, because of the discrepancies. Naturally, he concluded that his were correct, and the assistant's were wrong. At any rate the differences in observations were confounding their data. They were unable to achieve one unambiguous number by their traditional means. So they got rid of those errors, so-called, and by so doing, they also got rid of the human factor altogether. They introduced instruments which would give them unambiguous measures of events. They got rid of the individual awarenesses that I suggest contain the evidences of the human spirit! Their measures now are 'read' by a machine that provides the one unambiguous number that they prize. No evidence of the spirit could be obtained under such circumstances. By getting rid of the observers' errors—what you and I actually see became errors, errors!—they cut humans off from whatever spirit there was in their humanity for the purpose of obtaining their measures. However, by eliminating human inputs for physical ones, they may have done more than they know. They may have been "unguarded" once again in telling us such "facts" about our universe.

They appear not to have questioned whether their own physical measures themselves are not now biased due to eliminating just those human "errors," for they may have created new *physical biases* resulting from the instrumental means they initiated. Certainly, the machines will never disclose a spirit at work even if one were there! Theirs is surely one way of eliminating the human spirit! Unlike the experiments of psychology, where surplus results that I have interpreted as spirit do always occur, their bias is such that that *disclosure of the spirit can never take place in their data*. Of course, I do not really know if their instruments contribute a bias about the worlds they have now set before us as the real ones, but the nature of *their* physical world can only arise from those measures. We do not know whether what they have so measured is, indeed, the real world. It clearly is a world little affected by human influences. And it clearly is a world devoid of the human spirit. That some of them propose it is a universe in which we will not grow old if we travel at a fast enough pace, can only be a theoretical one. Is their world real or theoretical? A world bereft of the human spirit has to be a foregone conclusion in either event. The assumptions that physicists make, they should know by now, and some clearly do know that, do affect their measured outcomes.

Perhaps it does not matter that human beings when they look at the world—and that means also physicists—never could report what the measuring instruments of the physicists would report. But what they are omitting from their formulae may be exactly in the realm of that spirit which is never included in their theorizing. It is not included in their theorizing because it is left out of their observations and left out of their measurements. To theorize as I have done in Chapter IV requires that we never leave out the human equation—if equation is the proper word when looked at, for example, from my senior's perspective—because that 'equation' will always be an individual one. Furthermore, it is that very individuality that is prized in humanity, is it not?—though it is prized only in physics when that "human equation" is evinced in the genius of an Einstein, apparently.

Physical scientists are, and always have been, operating on the level of assumptions, and those assumptions come under the province of a psychology of awareness and consciousness rather than physics. Science actually begins with each scientist's awareness of the world which ultimately leads to his—or should I say, her—formulation of a view of the universe. Galileo began that process way back in the XVIIth century, and physicists have been following him ever since. What Galileo did, or perhaps it was just a thought experiment, was to consider just what happened when an object moved along an inclined plane compared to a level one. He noted that there would be an increase in acceleration as the movements became closer to the vertical downward. He noted that there were increases in acceleration as the object moved from a level plane to a vertical one. Then he thought,

'But what happens when the object moves from a level plane to one inclined increasingly upward?' He realized that in that case there would be deceleration with the strongest deceleration vertically upward. But then what one would have on level ground he concluded would be CELERATION!, for there neither ACceleration nor DEceleration would occur. Being a mathematician he cancelled out the AC and the DE—and was left with celeration. He *interpreted* that abstract, purely theoretical outcome as giving him the right to conclude constant motion: that a moving object, neither accelerating nor decelerating, would continue at that constant speed forever. In other words he concluded that abstraction which Newton then reinterpreted as the law of inertia. He concluded his theoretical result, not his actual result. He *denied absolutely the testimony of his senses that had always only seen objects in motion roll a bit and stop. He denied his sensory awarenesses for his abstract mathematical conclusion.*

Galileo began that process whereby sense observations were ignored by physicists now for a second reason. In addition to the unreliability of observers' eyes unaided by instruments, preference would always in the future be given to mathematical formulations over actual observations by the sense organs. Those two views, and the fallibility of the eyes of observers to provide objective data—data better determined by instruments and abstracted theoretical conclusions—would between them chart physics on the path it continues upon to this day. One outcome of that fact, and the new nature of theorizing, has been the formulation of my new Big Bang as entirely physical and as entirely theoretical. Their big bang is a conception, an idea, arising from a person's or some persons' psychological functioning. It is an idea which is an attempt—so far by physicists and astronomers working from an entirely physical base— to account for some of the facts that their observations have obtained. They do not actually know that there was anything like a big bang. It is an inference from observations made by their instruments. Their observations arise out of their psychological processes; and their conclusions arise out of their psychological processes. But their conclusions also arise out of their biased—that is biased from a human point of view—instrumentally based measurements and their abstracted way of drawing conclusions. These processes also include the unexpressed assumptions that could mean that their science is a bit "unguarded." This posssibility they appear so far to have overlooked. Overlooking that fact does not bode well for our understanding of what may have taken place way back there.

But the big bang—I guess I should not be capitalizing it in this context—is not an observation, but only a theory to account for some observations. And as I understand it, the observations now appear to raise questions about the theory's ability to predict, because some of the stars now appear to be older than the theoretical age of the theoretical big bang. I do not know what these oversights of observations and theorizing may mean for our views of the world. But an exploration of what the potential meanings could be appears to be a move in the right direction. That must be the case if we are truly to understand our places in the world and in the universe. It is also the stated aim and stance of science to be open to new ideas, and open to questions and doubts about traditionally accepted doctrines.

I admit that what I'm suggesting is speculative—speculative in the interests of coming to a more comprehensive formulation. I am asking these scientists to include the evidence, at least from the measurements of the observations of normal human beings to be incorporated into their theorizing. I speculate that that might someday result in a truly comprehensive theory. The human world and the physical world would somehow be included in one grand theory. Now *there* is a theoretical challenge! I cannot even speculate on whether or how that might be done. The speculations engaged in by some physicists on the other hand have been espousals of real nonsense, because they overlook the stubborn facts of the finiteness of human lives. The notion of space travel, for example, as recently espoused by Carl Sagan in his *Pale Blue Dot*, will never happen. His view that "We will begin to soar through the light years . . . and colonize the sky." is, it pains me to have to say, is absolute speculative nonsense. Because one of the theoretical conclusions of Einstein's theory results in, as I understand it, a reversal of time does not mean that we do not grow old in space travel no matter what its speed is. We are not on that purely theoretical time schedule. We live anchored in human time and in human space, not theoretical time and space, and we will live and die as humans must, in human time and in our three dimensional space. The fourth dimension is not real; it is a figment of a theoretical imagination. We will live out our span whatever the conditions, and that span is not great enough for even quite modest space flight—even to the nearest star and back. And many of us will live it as agonizedly as the college senior did as she thought her way to a conclusion that was central to her future existence. We are human beings, but we are also capable of a spiritual humanism that is denied by the current practices in physical science.

But living in human time rather than an idealized physical time, it will never be time that has *not* been infiltrated by the human spirit. Time does not arise in an awareness, but only in consciousness. Time and consciousness are allies. Space we can see and feel. Sometimes we can hear something like space—with an echo, for example. But time is not of the senses. And the physicists' space-time is not of the senses. It is an abstract, theoretical concept only. Time, itself, is a conception that only arises in humanity. And notice that it does not arise in very young children else they would not ask so often on trips whether we are there yet. Accordingly, time only arises as an awareness of another awareness: Time arises only out of consciousness. Time is more of the spirit than space is—though the results in Chapter IV indicate that space too is influenced by the human spirit. Time and memory enter us only through the realm of the spirit that arises through human consciousness. Even the mundane human spirit that I have outlined above, I think takes on a somewhat fuller character when it is a constituent part of time and memory. As I said, I am sure the human spirit is more than I have indicated, but as yet I am unable to specify just what more it is.

But the instrument based observations upon which physicists and astronomers erect their theories, and the abstracted and mathematized nature of that theorizing have not only removed them from the human equation, but have removed their observations and theorizing from any cognizance of even a totally human spirit. What that means should be something they should attempt to examine. I doubt that the rest of us can. The split that they have fostered between us and our lived awarenesses needs to be made explicit. I hope that they will do that. If they do that, then perhaps their speculations will not lead them to gross misconceptions about what is humanly possible. Then, perhaps too, psychology will be seen in its full impact as the human science which can include both the spiritual and the physical—at least in a modest fashion.

So I challenge those thoughtful mathematicians and physicists to reexamine what they do and how they do it, and most central of all, I challenge them to rethink their assumptions.

CHAPTER VII

Rewriting Human History

Though history books have always dealt with human history, that human history has been one that featured rulers and kings and their polititics and wars that they fought to conquer other peoples. That is a history of external events in the public world. What I envision here is a kind of history that is concerned with what is central to all people, not just those who have conquered and ruled. These are the values by which human beings have lived and the ways of thinking that have characterized them. It is an internal history that I have in mind, and it centers around consciousness. It is not only kings who had values; their peoples also had values, though these were seldom given much credence by their rulers. Alfred North Whitehead in *Adventures in Ideas* suggests that over the last couple of millenia there has been a change in human values which has replaced force with persuasion. He died before the atrocities committed by the Nazi regime had come to light, so I don't know whether he would have held to his earlier view. I think that there is still something to what he wrote despite the displays of force that characterized the Nazi treatment of the Jews. Even there, there was often a kind of persuasion—with force, of course, always ready to take its place. But in *The Nazi Doctors* Robert J. Lifton describes how at least some physicians were *persuaded* to commit acts that were atrocities. Of course, force probably was in the minds of those physicians as they were persuaded, so it makes for a confused point.

    I think, perhaps, that what Whitehead had in mind was the sorts of events that brought the Vikings onto British shores ravaging and pillaging the villagers. That kind of force had been used less, at least in the so-called civilized world. And there seemed to be more persuasion in the 1930s, perhaps, than now. And he knew nothing of the Holocaust, the Tutsis and the Hutus, and Bosnia. So I do not know how to place his conclusion any longer. But the rewritten history that I wish to set forth is of a different kind, anyway. I want to convey a kind of short history of the development of consciousness. First, how it arises in each person, and then how it may have arisen in the race. Then I want to consider just what the effects of what I view as changes in consciousness, and what the effects even in the development of consciousness may have upon humanity—considering the idea that it is consciousness that gives rise to the spirit in spiritual humanism.

Before anthropologists and archeologists became truly professional they sometimes referred to the people they studied as primitives. I prefer to call them primary peoples. They should be called primary peoples, because they live in a first hand or primary relationship with their surroundings. Once literacy has entered into humanity many of our awarenesses arise at second hand. Everything we read is an awareness taken indirectly from someone else's awareness, not from our own first hand experience. The experiences of primary peoples were all at first hand, rather than the second hand experiences that literacy has placed upon us. Our very young children's awarenesses of the world are at first hand; they too are primary persons, and so being, I think that every parent knows, that makes their experiences different from ours. The general and unprofessional view was that primary peoples were simply ignorant and confused in their beliefs, for they took seriously the power of spirits beyond themselves. How those views as primitive can be reconciled with the remarkable cave drawings that go back 30,000 years, it seems to me, should be more difficult than we have thought it to be, and I am sure, as all of the modern anthropologists now know it to be. I wish to reconsider all of those facts here. And perhaps considering those facts will lead us to a reconsideration of many of our views of what took place in human history.

Those caves include not only pictures of animals, not all of whom appear to have had practical significance as hunted animals, but in the most recent even older discoveries, also of human hands. It was not until about 3000 BC that writing was invented—and it was invented for practical reasons. When the sums of money in the ruler's coffers were held in the head of a priest who died, the accounting was much too difficult to be acceptable. But art was, I assume, impractical from its multi millenia earlier beginnings, and I say this despite the overwhelming number of people who think that their art was practical. But art is sometimes allowed to be impractical even now. And I believe that it always has been impractical at its base. I follow Whitehead in his views expressed in *Modes of Thought*:

> The central organism which is the soul of man is mainly concerned with the trivialities of human existence. . . . Instead of fixing attention on the bodily digestion of vegetable food, it catches the gleam of sunlight as it falls on the folliage. It nurtures poetry. Men are the children of the Universe with foolish enterprises and irrational hopes.

I say that art is of the human spirit, and the human spirit is not practical. Our bodies are practical. Language, too, I hold, like art, is of the spirit and began as impractical art-like expressions. It takes only the articulation of a breath to make artistic sounds as our singing shows. And our religious beliefs—well they are of the spirit, but they may have arisen and continue for practical reasons—in some cases, but not all. The journey of the spirit, especially awakened in consciousness, is the theme that is set forth in this rewriting of human history—that theme and its consequences.

Humanity's earliest times are really beyond any human records. I see no reason to assume that drawings did not exist before the ones in caves that have been discovered. When our son, Peter, was no more than ten months I drew the outline of a truck without the wheels, because I knew he was fascinated by trucks. He immediately scribbled whirling circles where the wheels belonged. That was just about the time that he came to his first names for things. I see no reason to assume that language has not been in existence at least as long as drawing—perhaps longer. Unlike the theory of evolution which sees so much of our outcomes as practical, my view of the evolution of consciousness is that it began in impracticalities—and may be continuing to do so. Language began, I suggest, as soon as the human brain came into existence with its current language centers in the left hemispheres, its highly developed frontal lobes with their symbolizing capacities, and with a long enough neck which included a larynx, and then a mouth with a tongue and lips, all attached to lungs to expell the breath that makes explicit and articulated sounds possible. Then as now, and as all three month-old babies do, the babies of the original homo sapiens would gurgle and coo. If the mother did not share in this set of mutations from the Neanderthalers, then nothing would happen. There are speculations about that the Neanderthalers lacked our language areas in the left hemisphere; there are other speculations that their necks were too short to make those distinguishing sounds that even our infants can make. Try saying cup and then coop noting where the hard c is placed in the mouth and throat. Such articulated sounds are part of our basic human repertoire even as infants along with our symbolizing capacities which our large frontal lobes and our language areas in the left hemispheres foster. How much acoustic response there would be to the cooing and gurgling would depend to some extent upon these factors.

At six to seven months this little baby would begin to babble—la, la, la, la, and da, da, da, da, and very likely, ma, ma, ma, ma, ma. To this day all babies who are not brain damaged go through this cooing-babbling sequence even if they are deaf. A deaf child was reported as saying: "Paka-paka-paka-paka," but in time that sounding out stopped. The babbling gradually disappears in deaf babies, because being deaf there is no response to their own sounds; the sounds do not turn into cultural sounding babbling, and finally speech, so the soundings simply disappear. In hearing babies, however, the babbling gradually takes on the flavor of the surrounding sounds: French, German, Chinese, English, and so on depending upon their surroundings. But I am back there before language began, so the child could not, and thus would not take on the qualities of the surrounding language. Did those people hum a lot? I ask, because I knew a little girl whose mother played music all day long, and her prespeech babbling involved a lot of humming. Babies pick up what is going on in the surroundings and incorporate whatever it is into their own expressiveness. Would it be the sounds of nature that these early people would mimic? We'll never know.

The origins of language here become dependent upon whether the mother is the beneficiary of the total set of mutations that make language possible: symbolizing processes, the language centers in the brain, the proper lips, tongue, larynx, and so on. If she does not have all of these, she may not respond, and then her daughter will not continue to make the articulated sounds and their nuances that lead to language. But if she has inherited all of the components of language, but her own babbling had fallen on ears that were unresponsive, *she* would be responsive to such sounds emanating from her daughter. She would, after all, be a very young half-child herself. And then, of course, she would play these sounding games with her baby—as we do to this day. These sounding games in time take on some stability. We forget them because they are not language, and are only on the way to what is important: language. Our son, Peter, my wife noticed, was sounding out "Toop-toop" as he lay on his stomach rocking back and forth. So she joined in this game, and in time I did too. It became so ingrained that the sounding itself would cause him to turn onto his stomach, rock, and sound out "Toop-toop." He emmitted other stabilized sounds as well, and I suggest that that little girl who, with her mother, originated speech in the human race, may have done so as well. Some sets of such child-mother teams would have done just that. This would make it the baby-mother theory of the origins of speech in the race.

But these stabilized sounds are not words. They are not even the names, the names that name one person or thing that I believe preceed words. These soundings are stable, but totally contextualized largely bodily expressions. In time, however, I can imagine that a girl or her mother noting the clumsiness of one of the communal boy babies bumbling about might simply ejaculate: "Bumblum!" Such reactions are not at all unusual in children and expressive people. When Peter had his first sip of an ice cream soda through a straw his immediate reaction was: "Fuzzeee!" And the expression: 'Bumblum' as a proper name might take hold and become attached to that boy. Similar onomatapoetic soundings would become the proper names for others. We had three cats, and our son was, of course, surrounded by language. Such happenings would simply be taken as a matter of course in those communal surroundings.

We called the cats such names as 'Kitty-cat,' 'Catty-cat,' 'Kitty-kitty,' and by their given names 'Cleo,' 'Sister,' and 'Himself.' One day on seeing all three cats march into the room together, an explosive "Kit-ten!" was released from Peter's mouth, but one could also say it came right out of his body. It was a wooden, clearly articulated name, indeed. Note that his name for the cats, for that is what it was, was his unique way of referring to them, for they were cats, not kittens, and we never referred to them as kittens—for that would have been incorrect. I call this a name because names name one thing—or in this instance one global experience. Names are singular. Peter's "Kitten" sounds as if it were general, but it was too early for him to distinguish singular and plurals. Names can name a global experience as the vague name-words in early languages indicate. Our words are general. Words name concepts which organize and relate diverse experiences. The word ocean, recall, organizes and identifies the huge, warm Pacific and the smaller, colder Arctic, and despite their vast differences makes them the same: oceans. Peter went on for a time with names. The second one was 'Bike' taught to him by his baby sitter. When he entered the path at the end of which the bicycles were stored he went into a paroxym of "Bike," "Bike," "Bike!"

But he did get to words, the words which remove us from direct experiences into more general and abstract ones—in time. And I knew for sure that he had arrived at words when one day he pointed to a kitchen chair and asked, "Dis?" I told him that it was a chair. Then he went into the living room and pointed at the high backed purple chair and asked, "Dis?" I said, "Chair." He nodded, and pointed at the coffee table. I said, "Table." He walked toward the dining area and pointed at the dining table. I said, "Table." We walked around the house in this fashion and he got the concepts of many household objects into his head as words. But how did our originating mother and daughter move from names to words? Just as the capacity was in Peter to move from names which name one event, to words which stand for an relate a variety of experiencings in one conception, so too was that capacity in the girl who helped to originate language. She would indicate things when she got to the point—around eighteen to twenty-one months—when the conceptualizing faculty had been reached. This capacity is true of all of us, and the mother and the daughter between them would have coined a few vague terms to which their generalizing propensities would have led them. It is a fact that what I call the movement from names to words shows an increase that is ten fold between eighteen and twenty-one months. It is simply in the nature of our thalamo-cortical systems that between eighteen and twenty-one months, it has developed to the point where it subserves generalized concepts.

And then, of course, the development of language, not just speaking, in the race would be able to move from its playful and, perhaps, its aesthetic or magical qualities, to more practical ones—and what is important—more theoretical ones. With the advent of the conceptualizing factor speaking becomes language, true language. I say that because rather than merely naming a person or a quality, propositions can be asserted even if they are merely one word assertions. The movement into those conceptions that referred to the world propositionally, more than merely to the persons in the surroundings, might well have been the impetus for the development of the magical and the mysterious—the development of the gods and religion. In *Language and Myth* Ernst Cassirer shows how language by its conceptual nature leads to religious beliefs, and how they gradually moved from beliefs in momentary gods to the highly conceptual one God of the more advanced religions. As time went by the intellectual power in words was also unleashed, and in time has led to the kind of thought that we know so well today—problem solving thought that is so bound up with rationality and science.

We know from anthropology that all cultures do not value the explicit concepts that we so admire. Their conceptions were vaguer than ours, and those original ones would have been like that, no doubt. The spirit and the material or the emotional and the physiological were not as separated then as they are for us who have inherited such clarity from the Greeks. For example, one of the primary cultures has a term "*mamichlapinatapai*" whose meaning approximately is, "looking at each other, hoping that each will offer to do something which both want but are reluctant to undertake." That is a general conception which is all merged with emotions, feelings of hope, and no doubt much more. We would not be likely to call it a concept, such as book is for us. The original language would be expressive with feeling meanings more than with cognitive meanings. Trobriand Islanders sighting land after a long voyage exclaim: "*Pwaypwaya!*" which meant, 'soil on which we tread and labor,' not our more abstract: "Land ho!" Their word was heavily laden with feeling and emotion, relief, prospect of rest, comfort, pleasure, and no doubt these were all intermingled in one global conception. It took millenia before the Western world sorted out its words as separable from feeling—if we have really done so even now. Our politicians certainly do not do so. After all those using the original languages were in no hurry, and anyway, they had millenia in which to develop a language which would better serve cognition. This latter development apparently depended upon the Greeks and on the development of their language. For, as I shall show, it is from them that the strengths and the weaknesses of our current conceptions arose.

When I published a version of my above theory of the origins of language in the race in *Current Anthropology* thirty years ago, one of the rebutting writers expressed astonishment that I could suggest that language arose by chance. I responded that I had not said that speech had arisen by chance, but that it had not arisen for any practical purpose necessarily, and furthermore, was not, as they were suggesting, developed for practical purposes as a means of communication that would foster our survival. I still suggest that language originally did not have a practical purpose, though it plainly has one now at times—

though it is more often used for the practical purpose of obfuscation than it is for the practical purpose of communication. But isn't poetry expressive rather than communicative—in the sense of communicating information? Now I would say that language arose as our finest means of expressing in a spirited and symbolic way what matters most to us. Perhaps that was its original purpose; we'll never know.

In *Modes of Thought* Alfred North Whitehead said, "The account of the sixth day should be written, He gave them speech, and they became souls." That consciousness through which we have a sense of a human soul is no doubt aided by the fact that we have language. Language is likely to have added to our sense of having another being within us so that an inner dialogue could take place. Our developed language allowed us to arrive at clear-cut concepts as well as those vaguer conceptions that all of us employ still almost all of the time. We can now even use language with the aim of theorizing. We can now also use language to praise God. And we can now use language to criticize art. I am not prepared to assume that it arose for those purposes, however. I believe that language arose pretty much as I have just described the process. But language has certainly been for many, at least, a witness to the spirit of the universe. "In the beginning was the Word . . . and the Word was God," is merely one example. Language, along with art, has been a major means of witnessing, of bearing witness to the human spirit—and that Spirit that was there, for all we can know, when the physicists' big bang occurred?

The civilizations of Egypt and Mesopotamia antedate all others in our Western world. Though they formulated very different world views, both included a sense of something that I would call spirit. The spiritual quality was evident in their reacting to their environments as if they were facing a 'Thou' rather than an 'It.' They were reacting to another being as enspirited as themselves. We have lost that sense to the point where even human beings may not now be treated as another thou. There was no place for something as dead as an 'It' in those highly developed ancient cultures. The Greeks, coming later, had their gods and their thous too, and the Hebrews had theirs. The spirit had always been given a religious tinge, both in those civilized cultures and those less civilized. Even today that remains the case, for as I understand it some ninety-four percent of the citizens of the United States profess a belief in God. What I am calling the human spirit has a very complex constitution, for I theorize that it arose from and consists of expressivity, appurtenance, and a symbolizing factor—at least. And the spirit is evidenced in us in our human registrations, in our awarenesses, and especially in our highly developed consciousness, and in our reflective consciousness. But the spirit that I mean to establish has an entirely human face. It would have to be another Spirit that would have the possibility of being existent beyond humanity. In other words it is not a spirit based necessarily upon a belief in a deity. That Spirit may, indeed, exist apart from human beings, but if It does Its composition is unknowable by us. I suggest, though, that if It does exist, It is likely to be of a complexity greater than our own. Our human spirit arises, I believe, out of our consciousnesses. More than that I don't know.

Our spirit, which has had its outcome in the various religions, is not merely an ephemeral epiphenomenon, but involves a complex admixture of what matters to us arising out of our natural expressivity; both of these are transformed by our symbolizing powers. It is these symbolizing powers which provide us with that sense of another being within us. This admixture of components is what also gives rise to our awareness of a problem or a need for a decision in our everyday lives. Then we begin to reflect, and this reflection has to involve what I call consciousness. It is one aspect of our reflective consciousness that led to rational thought. I see that as beginning in the Western world with Socrates and culminating in the scientific revolution in the 17th century. But its process remained so unclear that John Dewey wrote a book on reflective thought in the 1930s—*How We Think*. One sense of consciousness led to thought, theory and rationality. Another sense of consciousness led to consciences and human values. Another sense of consciousness emphasized the aspect that called up its non sensory character as a kind of ephemeral experience within us. That latter sense of consciousness is so different from our usual sensual experience that it often has been called spiritual, and it, along with language appears to be the basis of positing a soul in human beings. This personal experience of the spirit, however, is ours only, and is not to be foisted upon the universe. Whatever that may be that may have been there from the beginning of the big bang is also what I have been calling Spirit for want of a better term. It is an apt and appropriate term for our personal experience; it is bound to be a misnomer for whatever It may be that may have been an immeasurable component of the Big Bang. How the big bang became an unspirited and neutered *it* needs its historical examination, so that we can move beyond where we have been mired for so long. Surely the uninspired nature of the big bang took a powerful separation in consciousness of our feelings from our thinking.

In *The Discovery of the Mind* Bruno Snell tells us that it was out of the body of the Greek language that science arose. Specifically, it was the definite article "*the*" which he proposes was central to the rise of science. Snell says:

> The single lion to which I refer by adding the article, is the object of a statement: 'The lion is old.' Like a name, the concrete noun preceded by the definite article specifies a particular object which *is* lion. Now the generic article has this function that it makes this original statement the object of a new statement. *The* lion, as a scientific concept, comprises the sum total of everything that *is* lion. Thus a new concept is posited. 'The lion' differs from 'the lions' or simply 'lions' in that its existence extends beyond the empirical concrete race of lions, and that, in spite of the singular, it comprehends all known or knowable lions.

This new *generalized* lion, *the* lion, need strike fear into no one! He is not present; he is never present; he never has been present; he does not exist; he is as abstract as any scientific concept. He is as abstract as the law of inertia—so-called—which is a proud successor to the Greek invention of abstractions, though inertia was proposed more than two millenia later.

People apparently forget that the so-called laws of physics are often phantoms. The law of inertia states: An object in motion will continue in motion at the same speed and in a straight line forever. It is seldom stated that nothing on earth can actually occur according to the so-called law. The law of inertia cannot occur in our solar system, the only system Galileo knew, because all motions are subject to a gravitational force which forces them away from a straight line and/or into a change in speed or direction. The law of inertia has been called a 'rape of the senses,' because no such motion had ever been seen to occur, nor could it occur. Yet its abstract formulation served a useful scientific purpose for almost three centuries. It became one of the foundations of Newtonian physics. That is our direct legacy from the Greek language and thought. When a lion has become a nonexistent general concept the way to science could begin. It is not surprising that out of their thought and their unique language they could invent an *it*. For it is an *it* upon which science depends. Science has to deal with objectified phenomena. All of the phenomena from psychological laboratories that I cited in a previous chapter became objectified through measurement just as have the facts of physics been so constructed. And all of these objectifications had to wait until an *it* was invented before physics could be formulated theoretically.

And that *it* was given its fullest power in the "unbelievable" instrumental world that the physicists of the seventeenth century created.

According to Owen Barfield in *Romanicism Comes of Age,* Rudolf Steiner dubbed the era up until about 1450 the Intellectual Soul. I believe that that period is better called the Age of Intelligence, for intelligence was, indeed, what was being displayed by the Romans and others from that time onward. Since 1450 we should have been enjoying what I call the Age of Consciousness. But it is intelligence which is still the most salient feature of modern thought—not consciousness, not yet. In physics and astronomy Kepler and Galileo were using their intelligence to pave the way for Newton to formulate his so-called laws of motion well after the end of that age. And all of that was happening even as Shakespeare was initiating the Age of

Consciousness with his play *Hamlet* around 1600. Consciousness had, of course, been operating to enhance problem solving, scientific theorizing, and intelligence and rationality in general, but consciousness marked a new emphasis that arose as a central issue at about that time. I believe that our intelligence is wearing thin in these early centuries of the Age of Consciousness. We need to place more reliance on consciousness than upon intelligence during our current age which according to my understanding has more than half a millenium remaining in it. I find that it is failures of consciousness that are now interfering even with the operation of intelligence.

Consciousness is needed to think our way through to a theory of physics, but a new consciousness that includes values apart from the self, a guage of what matters beyond *self* satisfaction or *self* agrandizement, true feelings of value, are what become paramount in the Age of Consciousness in which we now live. I suggest that in the Age of Consciousness a new spirit can arise. It is the feelings of value which can be embodied in a spiritual humanism.

I have offered a definition of human feeling: An emotion that comes under the control of the frontal lobes of the cerebral cortex so that reflection can enter and form a conception of what matters to us as a personally and deeply felt value. One kind of consciousness was needed to initiate and carry forth theorizing thought in the Age of Intelligence. A new form of consciousness is now needed to initiate and carry forth the valuing expressed in feelings that are appropriate for the Age of Consciousness. Though the conceptions about what matters are similar to the concepts of a theory, the two have very different aims. The aim of feeling is to arrive at just what value is paramount in this specific situation so that a proper action can be taken. Thinking aims at relating diverse entities and uniting them under one comprehensive set of concepts. Note how diverse the entities were that Newton and then Einstein related into grand theories. Feeling, however, is tied to its context or to an actual situation; thinking aims at a generality that is contextless. The two, thinking and feeling, however, are not opposites; they are complementary. We need both. But I believe that too much of our thinking has been bereft of the feeling that sets our human values. As important as theorizing is, it really would not be all that beneficial to humanity to restrict ourselves to theorizing without considering what really matters to us human beings. And yet that is what we have been doing. Intelligence was not lacking in Germany during Hitler's regime.

Feelings have been denigrated as mere emotionality. But that will no longer do. In the Age of Consciousness the basic priority of human feelings of value are central spiritual qualities for the advent of the new spiritual humanism. We are not prey to our momentary impulses once we have consciousness. And being able to reflect upon our own reflections is a function of that consciousness. Rationality, too, is an outcome of that same consciousness, but in our age of the centrality of physical science that aspect of consciousness has been given a great deal of emphasis. Our feelings have not been concentrated upon to the same extent as our thought has. Feelings, when we feel about events rather than emotionalize them, are clear expressions of the human spirit. Feeling and consciousness are central components of the new spiritual humanism that I am espousing.

The role of consciousness in our time is as a helping spirit to aid us in determining how to conduct ourselves in the world. Penrose and the adherents of AI miss the depth of the role that consciousnesss plays in helping us to formulate our human values. Though Penrose envisions a positive role for consciousness beyond the one that the AI people can conceive, his remains tied to thinking rather than feeling. As a result his view of consciousness is truncated in comparison with the role consciousness actually plays, and with what a fuller consciousness can play in humanity's future. Consciousness contains and engenders the spirit which brings our sense of human values to the fore, and expands their role. Consciousness is the bearer of the means for arriving at the values possible for human beings in the Age of Consciousness. We have always lived our lives based on values of one sort or another. Now we can more clearly assess values and form them out of the consciousness which we possess as human beings in the new Age of Consciousness.

CHAPTER VIII

Spiritual Humanism

Spiritual humanism is silent upon just what it was that made up the original source that might well have included both the physical and the spiritual dimensions in one. It is silent there because we cannot know Its characteristics. But we can know the characteristics of our new spiritual humanism. Its major qualities involve the employment of consciousness to establish through reflection our rational thought and our individual human values. The human feelings which give witness to our values play a major role in enspiriting our humanistic inclinations, and these are fostered by the consciousness that we can bring to bear on these issues. We do not need to educate children to values—the home and religious organizations are the places for those—but we do need to introduce them, and everyone else, to using their own reflective processes to employ their consciousnesses to consider just what matters to them, and just what matters to humanity more generally. That does mean that children can be introduced to valuing in school, because there are bound to be circumstances where clashes of values arise. Educators can use those opportunities to examine values, just as they use opportunities to examine thoughts. The basic tenets of this new spiritual humanism include the education of feeling values at least as highly as we have for so long valued the education of thinking.

The spirit in spiritual humanism arises from our awarenesses and our consciousness which have given us the sense of a soul-like being within us. The humanism arises from the fact that our concerns are with the human condition, human values, and the values that human beings are capable of having. I have no quarrel with those who espouse deistic views, but I want to establish a place for those who have a deep feeling for, a valuing of the possibilities in the spiritual side of our human lives, but have little or no outlet for it in current religious forms—people like myself. I find it difficult to understand, given the fact of how little we know, or can ever know of the beginnings of the universe and of our humanity, how some people subscribe to atheism. We do not and cannot really know enough, I believe—ever to come with certainty to that conclusion. Consequently, I would conclude that such an assumption, and/or conclusion, is itself an act of faith. It has to be an act of faith, because none of us, neither I nor they have, nor can have the final intellectual information which would allow us to subscribe definitively to that view, or to any other doctrinaire view. My intellectual view on those matters is outlined in the introductory chapter. I have more to say on that here.

It seems to me that knowing as little as we do, it is unlikely that the physical big bang sufficiently covers what took place back there. I believe that it involves considerable *hubris* even to think that we could know that the event was only physical in our current terms. I cannot believe that any of us, not privy to divine revelation, can know what might have been there. My own sense of it is of a kind of Force that may even be greater than the physical big bang. It could be much broader in scope than what physicists with their narrow instrumentally based findings have been assuming. A "Force" that is probably some admixture that could include our physical and what I am calling the spiritual, but perhaps well beyond those is what I have in mind. But that that "Force" has any real awareness of us and our little world, or of me and my piddling concerns, I seriously have to doubt. But atheism is a faith to which I cannot subscribe, because we simply cannot *know* that there was and is only the physical, as we currently define it, and nothing of any spirit there.

My views that are based upon my own feeling values and what I can now conceive of are another matter. And though I am not really sure that I even now know altogether what the totality of all of my views comprise, they are completely humanity oriented and humanistic to the core. One serious difference that can arise from a deistic as opposed to a humanist orientation is that morality can overpower and, perhaps, even obliterate what should be decided on the basis of ethical considerations. The other serious difference, and it really is a danger, is that our true spiritual quality will go unrecognized, because it is not a religious spirituality. These two issues are the central concerns of this chapter. The differences between morality and ethics will be considered first, because that is at the core of the matter of spiritual humanism. With those differences clarified, the problem of the spiritual as part of a humanistic spiritual attitude becomes at least in the way of being resolvable.

It is consciousness that helps to differentiate morality from ethics. Consciousness refers to any reflection upon our awareness of any other thing or event. Such reflections are not experiences that are at all alien to us once we have achieved our adult consciousness. When consciousness applies to any and all events in awareness, especially those apart from us and our usual self interests, then it is clear that when I am aware of another person's suffering, that awareness exists apart from whether or not I am involved in that suffering. I may, of course, empathize with their suffering and then I have become somewhat personally involved, but I can also be aware without having to be involved. Personal involvement becomes something that is in the power of the person to some extent to regulate depending upon how the situation enters into what matters to him or her, or whether it engages a peripheral or one of their central values.

This consciousness, however, gives us the ability to some extent to be in control of our reactions so that we can also be *disinterestedly interested* in whatever it is that engages our interest. That ability, it seems to me, has been one that has been with us as a possibility at least from the time of Socrates. Socrates pioneered the increasing rationality which arose from what seem to me to have been disinterested interests. From that time on some form of disinterested interest was evident in the Greek spirit. Do the newly discovered cave paintings also indicate that ability to be disinterestedly interested? Would it be that in art our *disinterested interest* first occurred? Socrates displayed a clear ability to consider events in their own terms apart from their effect upon him. He engaged the issues of his time in a way which almost totally displayed a lack of self interest. Even his approaching death was dealt with by him in a *interestedly disinterested* manner. Despite the nearly two and one-half millenia that have passed since then, we appear to have lacked a definition of consciousness and its disinterested interest that could make those so evident human abilities clear to humanity. Our perspective on our humanity has been narrowed, I believe by the lack of awareness of such central concepts as a consciousness that has a place for disinterested interests in our human relations with one another.

This important facet of consciousness that has so long remained undefined is what has a clarifying effect upon the differences between morality and ethics. A little story may clarify matters here. The secretary for a group of us faculty members mentioned to me one day that she was taking a course in ethics at the local college—she knew that I had philosophical interests. In the course of our discussion she said, "Well, I don't believe in abortion, but I wouldn't feel right in deciding about that for another person." I knew that she was a practicing Roman Catholic, so I found this a refreshing point of view. Since I had been dealing with just this issue in my own writing, I suggested to her that as I saw it she was taking an ethical position rather than a strictly moral one on the issue of abortion. She was *not* foisting upon others her personal moral standards, but was willing to allow them to have and to live by their own moral standards despite her lack of agreement with them. This meant to me that she was using her consciousness to take a personally disinterested, but still a deep interest in the issue. Such disinterested interests is what allows us to entertain ethical, rather than merely moral ones. I think the difference between ethics and morality has useful implications for all of us, not only about abortion, but about many issues. This one of abortion, however, appears to be a central issue in our time.

The moral injection: "Thou shalt not kill" appears to many anti-abortionists to apply even to the youngest human embryo. As a result of that view they see both abortionists, and any women who seek abortions, as murderers. This view I take to be a moral one. It appears to have arisen originally from a religious source, one that may have resulted from revelation. It is applied by the anti-abortionists regardless of any mitigating circumstances. For the commandment having come from their Deity, they believe that it is to be applied no matter what the circumstances. Mitigating circumstances are apparently deemed irrelevant. The consciousness involved in such a conclusion is narrowed to one: their personal conscience based on their God's injunction to man—and to woman, and to woman especially.

That this view is one that is applied to people other than themselves is attested to by the fact that many of the major anti-abortionists are men. Their justification has to be the injunction of their religion, because it is not an outcome that could ever be applied to them. Though, accordingly, they could never truly assess their own reactions caught in the circumstances of a woman seeking an abortion, they apply their moral standard to her in an absolute fashion. None of the mitigating circumstances of the relations within which the woman seeking an abortion may be entertaining could possibly enter into their absolute standard of evaluation. The anti-abortionist demonstrates an attitude that ignores the relationships within which the woman seeking an abortion is exposed to, and by which she may have finally come to what may well be for her personally the most momentous decision of her life. Research indicates that seekers of an abortion, most often feel that it is an extremely serious decision. The same can well be true for their view of those physicians who are willing to provide abortions. The anti-abortionists deem them murderers without considering the physicians' network of their own relationships, and individual moral codes and ethical beliefs, or the sincere view that the work being done is for humanitarian reasons. In all such instances there is a failure to utilize the abilities resident within every human being's consciousness that allows some, at least, to disengage themselves from personal and absolutist moral concerns to consider the relative ethical ones that a person other than ourselves may be entertaining.

By relative standards I do not mean, however, to suggest at all that everything is relative in some simplistic sense. It is instead the case that ethical standards as opposed to moral ones are those that can consider the network of relations, and the set of relationships within which another person is operating. And since these can only be known by the one in that situation, it is reasonable from an ethical position to allow those persons to come to their own moral judgements about their own actions. For it is a moral judgement for the person coming to a decision about whether to have or not to have the abortion. They have to face whatever moral set of injunctions they have lived by in coming to that decision. In everything that I have read, it is a terribly difficult decision for most women to make. How it can be equally difficult for any man to face is clearly impossible; yet this great discrepancy goes entirely overlooked. It is a not a moral decision for the men themselves, but it is their morality which they apply indiscriminately to women, because for the man personally the decision cannot morally be personally either right or wrong. That personal moral issue is inapplicable and therefore irrelevant to them. I suggest that the women have the right to be treated as in an ethical as well as in a moral delemma, both of which they may know too well personally. But the anti-abortionists' appear to insist that the moral standard set, they believe, by their religion must have precedence in every instance.

If we could learn to restrict moral judgements to our own actions and to our own decisions, and apply ethical judgements to situations and, especially, to persons apart from us, then we would all be using the capacity that our consciousness does provide for all undamaged, adult human beings. For that consciousness that arises in childhood is present in some form in all intact human beings. That we have not been taking cognizance of that ability does not mean that its potentiality has not been there all along. It is also that quality in consciousness which allows us to operate within the realm of interests other than self interests. It is the source of that disinterested interest to which I referred earlier.

Ethics always requires a differentiated consideration of the others' network of relationships upon which judgements about their decisions need to be made. Morality involves only the relations between persons and their own beliefs. In most cases it also involves their relations to their religious doctrines. Morality applied to another person usurps the moral code by which that person lives. Moral injunctions applied to others requires that they conform to an alien moral code, one alien to them, that is. Moral standards applied to another person are an invasion of that person's own set of moral standards. Our human history is full of examples of the use of moral strictures upon persons who did not adhere to them. The Inquisition is only a major example of that. With the consciousness available to humanity the application of alien moral standards could no longer be the potent factor it has always been. If we would, indeed, allow to others the ethical right to their own moral codes and their own beliefs, and to the consequences of their actions taken on those beliefs, many of the difficulties still facing us in this so-called post modern world could be solved. The ethical position gives the locus of decision to the individual and removes it from outsiders who cannot know the moral code, or other moral concerns of the person making the decision.

I suppose that it could be argued that abortion involving as it does the termination of a human existence resides in a different realm from purely humanistic concerns. It could, therefore, be concluded that it resides in its own perculiarly singular niche. And life and death matters are more important than all others. Once a life has been terminated, it is over irrevocably. That is why I am personally against the death penalty. The finality of death is a fact. That is, I believe, the reason why so many persons of a humanistic bent reject the application of the death penalty. Many societies, at least in modern times, have recognized mitigating factors which take into account the individual person's network of relations and circumstances within which the death occurred. In acting in this fashion, those societies that do so are acting on ethical grounds according to this distinction, for they consider the relationships holding within the circumstances surrounding the death rather than holding the person to an absolute moral injuction: "Thou shalt not kill." Or if you do, then you must also be killed.

Even granting then the signal importance of life, the distinction between ethics and morality allows us to gauge the difference between holding others to moral versus ethical standards. Despite the importance of the life of any human being, a distinction between ethics and morality can aid us in coming to a conclusion about the outcomes of our beliefs. Those outcomes become more humane and more in the spirit of humanism as they allow each person the latitude to apply moral judgements to themselves and ethical ones to others.

Spiritual humanism espouses ethics over morality. It asks each of us to treat all others with respect for their points of view. This does not mean that it condones criminal behavior, but it does mean that it is incumbent upon us that we look at the total context surrounding the criminal act—both the person who commits it and the surrounding environment within which it was committed. Of course we are all interested in justice, but complete self interest can be replaced in spiritual humanism by a kind of disinterested *self* interest as well as a disinterested interest in all that goes on. The removal of ourselves as the total center of everything is one outcome of adhering to the tenets of the new spiritual humanism.

It could be objected, I suppose, that the spirit in spiritual humanism is somewhat attenuated compared to the kinds of religious ectasy that have been associated with religions in the past. I don't believe that that need be so or that it is so. The human spirit in the sense of our consciousness of our own consciousness has been increasing even in the many millenia that our awarenesses could be interpreted as involving consciousness. We have, however, most often used our consciousness to foster intelligence, rather than our values. Our values as children often revolve around satisfying bodily needs and egocentric interests. It is only with adulthood that we can hope to espouse those *other oriented values* that can mark the highest possibilites of feeling in human beings. The spirit of the anti-abortionists despite their proclaimed aims has fostered anger and enmity. They proclaim the sanctity of life, even some of their religions proclaim the sanctity of life, when they both should be fostering the sanctity of the souls of people—where the spiritual quality that pervades life through our consciousness resides. It was the depth of the soul that Heraclitus proclaimed; it is the depth of the soul which is the central nature of spiritual humanism. Life does not have the depth that is possible in the human soul, or the depth of feeling that is dependent upon the human soul. It is not the soul as it is defined by religions of which I am speaking; it is the soul defined in terms of its depth of feeling, by the extent of its own self awareness and consciousness applied to the circumstances of living. The soul is different from the mind, for the soul has to do with feeling values rather than with thought and intelligence. Both feeling and thinking involve reflecting upon things; As thought requires reflective thinking, feeling requires reflection upon emotional circumstances. It is the humanistic feeling soul that prevents it from being satisfied with mere intelligence. It is by its good intentions toward the feeling and value side of humanity that spiritual humanism is best defined. Religions that foster the sacredness of life have forgotten their task which is to nurture and to foster the deepest aspects of humanity—the souls of every living human being.

Spiritual humanism means to foster the life of the soul—the soul of each human being that may go beyond even this newly defined consciousness. It takes seriously Nicholas of Cusa's conclusion that if we accept that no one can ultimately know God, then we could all agree that God is one—equally unknown and unknowable to all and by all. Spiritual humanism also takes seriously the possibility that we cannot know that the big bang was an entirely physical event. Furthermore, it concludes that the spiritual aspect of the soul is not necessarily reducible to psychology's consciousness, nor to the formulation I set forth in chapter IV, though for all we can now know, that may be the case. We can, however, utilize ethical instead of moral injunctions when we make decisions about human beings other than ourselves. Spiritual humanism is willing to conclude that there is much that we do not know and cannot know, can never know about the nature of the lively force that set off everything, and seems even now to continue the evolution of humanity. The unknowable power that has unleashed our universe, and the billions of souls now resident in it, that power which we cannot know, deserves, I believe, a better treatment than the petty wars and enmities that fill our earth—in His name.

CHAPTER IX

Self Determinations

Self determinations have nothing to do with the theological idea of free will nor with the scientific notion of determinism. I have nothing as lofty as the former, nor nothing as mundane as the latter in mind at all. I call the former lofty because it is an assumption about human nature that our religions have to assert, else their exhortations to us to repent and to change our ways, never could be applied. And I call the latter mundane because the sciences have to assume that the events with which they deal are determined, else they would have to close down their enterprises. Without the assumption of determinism, the sciences would never have become what they are. They have to assume determinism of the events in our universe else they could never hope to determine the formula which would account for them.

Self determinations are at one and the same time both lofty and mundane, however. They are lofty because it is only in creatures with a well developed consciousness that self determinations can occur. It takes reflection, and even some dedication, not to be the plaything of impulses, and to be able truly to determine one's actions. But they are also mundane because self determinations are an ordinary human accomplishment. All such determinations require are people with consciousness who also wish to be capable of determining their actions themselves.

In Chapter IV I provided some proposals that explained some psychological phenomena in laboratory settings. There I accepted, and had to make the assumption that certain events are and can be determined; the events that occur under the controlled conditions of a laboratory are, I believe exceptions to the general rule that human events cannot be determined by a science. For there the observers in the experiment give over a portion of their ability to determine events temporarily to the experimenter for his or her purposes—not their own. But there I specifically omitted the events of everyday life from the general assumption of determinism. There is no evidence at all that the events in the lives of adult human beings are determined by, or can otherwise be determined by, any science. It is only by confusing the deterministic *assumption* that sciences use for the purpose of laboratory events, with those indeterminate everyday actions, that that issue could arise. I suggest, however, that to some extent we make of our lives what we put into them, so that we can to some extent determine them—excepting, of course, those myriad circumstances beyond our control. These circumstances include acts of nature such as floods and earthquakes, circumstances of birth such as neurological defects, poverty, early abuse, dire external circumstances, and all kinds of handicaps that cannot be overcome. But for adults in less dire circumstances, once adulthood has been achieved, the possibilities for beginning to determine aspects of one's life can be present.

Note that the word "determinations" in the title of the chapter is plural. By that I mean that *event by event* we can determine to arrive at *terminations* of whatever those situations are that face us. I believe that we can be successful at terminating such events much of the time. I also try to show in the chapter that such event by event practice of determinations can lead to an overall increase in our ability to determine events in our lives. A little story can be useful in illustrating the kind of self determinations I have in mind. I recall traveling as a passenger with a young woman colleague, who was the driver on a journey that was to take several hours. We inadvertently got onto the topic of accidents. Suddenly, she said, "If we don't stop talking about accidents, we are bound to have one." So, I thought, "It's up to me to do something." I searched among my awarenesses for a topic we shared, and I recalled reading an article that contained an item bordering on her field that I had meant to broach to her. I broke the silence by saying, "I have been meaning to ask you about a finding I read a couple of days ago," and though I no longer remember what it was, the change in topic worked to get us off the issue of accidents. It brought her into the area of her professional expertise, and she forgot her worry about accidents. I had meant to change the subject from accidents, I *determined* to do so, and I thought of a topic I had meant to broach, because it was within her area of interests. I broached *the topic* and brought the accident topic to an end. I *terminated* that topic, and it did not return during our whole trip. I *de-termined* the course of those events.

I suggest that what I just described is not all that unusual in adults. I also do recall picking up a young couple hitchiking thinking they were students from my college. They were not. The young man could not leave the topic of hitchikers holding up drivers; nor could I think how to change the subject. I was much relieved when I deposited them where they were going. But my failure there does not mean that we can *never* determine what we can and cannot do. We are fallible humans, or at least I am. What I mean is that we can to some extent determine our own actions—not anyone elses, surely. We can do that because, as is the case for all adult human beings, we possess a reflective consciousness. With consciousness we can consider our values, and think about what to do in a particular situation. Then, as we examine all of the opportunities in our awareness that are at our disposal, we can then somehow determine which action we take.

In *The Nazi Doctors* Robert J. Lifton documents how physicians who at first drew back from commiting atrocities, by being forced to be present during the aborent activities undertaken by others, gradually became accustomed to them, and in time assumed those tasks themselves. I imagine that they felt that they could not refuse to be there, and my guess is that their feeling might have been correct. Theoretically they did not have to act upon those bases, though the level of intimidation, and their own fears of reprisal, were clearly of great intensity. I suggest that it is possible for us to develop the attitudes, and the life skills, so that we can in time have some power over our lives—but never total power. We can determine—to what extent I do not know—but to some extent, we can decide what we will and will not do. And then we do or do not do it.

It is our consciousness, and especially our reflective consciousness, that gives us the powers that allow us to make our own decisions event by event in our lives. Given the fact that we can reflect upon our awareness in full consciousness of the outcomes that are possible, we can make our decisions on how to act in each specific instance. I gave a signal example of that with the college student in Chapter V, because it was the function of Educational Interchanges to provide the opportunity for reflection that could allow her to determine just what she would do in that important decision about her future life. Since consciousness is part of such a determining power, we can decide to act on the basis of human values, that is, on the basis of our own set of human values. Her value that led her to act as she did was the need to maintain her independence for her feeling of selfhood, even as she appeared to be giving in to the wishes of others. It is consciousness which makes a valuing life possible, and our determination to live life on such a basis arises from the fact of human consciousness.

I noted that Jung proposed that feeling tells us the values of things, and that feeling, like thinking itself, is a rational function. I think we would all agree that thinking is rational, but I also believe that many of us would still consider feeling to be too emotionally tied to be a rational function. What does distinguish feeling from emotion, and, of course there is no absolute demarcation here, is that the reflection that arises in consciousness can be brought to bear on emotional situations, just as they can be on non emotional ones—providing that the emotion does not run too high, however. Jung's standard for telling an emotion from a feeling was whether the physiological function was sufficiently brought into play. I would suggest that rage is an emotion as is the state of delerium, for in them no rational process is possible. Insofar then as a rational, reflective process can be brought to bear upon an emotional experience and affect that experience, I believe that we can call it a feeling. Love at first sight might be one of our better exemplars of this definition. The first sight may bring on an emotion, but with the second and third sights and so on, the emotion may have turned into a feeling. Maurice Merleau-Ponty speaks of the mysterious change we may experience of finding that what had been desire becomes a feeling of love. I suggest that that so common occurence is a movement from an emotion to a feeling. The feeling then tells us what matters to us, what the proper value of this person is, why we wish to be near her, and why we wish to retain her positive evaluation of us.

Jung believes that feeling and thinking are opposed. To a certain extent, I think he is right. If one decides, as Einstein did, that constructing a physical theory is the most important intellectual enterprise, it does not leave much room for considering just what it is that is most important as one passes through life. The major decision had already been made. That does not mean that he was not faced with what the value of this or that enterprise was daily, but the central one was never questioned. And I think he might have given less thought to each of those others as a result. Einstein was a thinking type in Jung's terms. A true feeling type would never have come to his original conclusion in the first place. The conclusion of the thinking type obviates the need for considering the alternatives that might have arisen in the course of life, and, indeed, would have already precluded them.

So just as consciousness brings with it the ability to reflect on events, the reflection can move in the direction of thinking with a theory as a possible result, or in the direction of feeling with evaluations about how we should act in our daily lives, and our lives in general, as the possible result. With our consciousness we can think about and reflect upon events, and we can, indeed, come to a conclusion about how we shall live our lives. If we dedicate our lives to feeling, we would consider the values involved in the life decisions we make. If we dedicate our lives to thinking, we might consider the theories we make about our human existence. But it seems to me that valuing itself may be the more important enterprise.

Neither consciousness nor values have held a high place in the intellectual lives of our generations since the turn of the past century. The pleasure principle has even been proposed as the basis for our actions. That formulation denies feeling values as a basis for human actions. And to deny that we can live by a set of values denies both the reality of our consciousness and our humanity. It also denigrates the humanity and the, at least, potential humaneness of our human spirit. Intelligence and rationality have held the center stage of human actions for far too long. It is time that the dramatic interest change to a concern with feelings of value which are as much, if not more, a function of the spirit in consciousness as is thought and rationality.

So far, however, I have been dealing with the events that have been determined *by* the self. More important than they, I think, are determinations *of* the self, determinations of what one will become even in the process of becoming it during a lifetime. I present as an example the following two determined women who could be said to have initiated what has become modern dance. There were forebears, of course. Isadora Duncan was one, and Ruth St. Denis and Ted Shawn, who founded the Denishawn Dancers, were others. From that remarkable company Martha Graham and Doris Humphrey, after they each individually separated from it, between them, largely determined the later course of modern dance in America.

These two women were born less than a year and one-half apart, Graham on May 11, 1894 and Humphrey on October 17, 1895. They had, however, very little contact with one another as Denishawn dancers, for Martha Graham worked almost exclusively with Ted Shawn and Doris Humphrey similarly, largely with Ruth St. Denis. Louis Horst, the composer of music for dance, played the music for Martha Graham's audition, and is reported to have said something like, 'I don't know if she is a dancer, but she certainly is a performer.' And when Doris Humphrey completed her audition, Ruth St. Denis is reported as asking, "What do you do?" Doris answered, "I teach dance." "You should be dancing." The former became a great dancer, and a noted choreographer; the latter became a great choreographer, and a dancer of note. Those are my opinions after watching films of both, and reading widely about them. Both were persons of powerful determination who determined the lives they were to lead, and, I believe, also determined the artists and persons they were to become. The two dancer-choreographers became ultimately, I believe selves that were ones that they determined to become, and so became.

Martha Graham began as a performer, and though she remained an incredible performer all of her long life, she became a dancer who could do things through moving her body that no one else seemed or seems able to do. The impact of her *Lamentation* of 1930, though I have only seen its filmed depiction of mourning, hits so strongly physically that the experience is truly bodily felt. At least for me it had a more powerful effect, almost, than any lived through real experience that I have undergone. Maybe it is my lack, or perhaps it is just something beyond most men, but that was the most emotion rending set of movements that I have ever witnessed. Since undergoing that I have also watched some of the filmed dances in which she danced, and her later choreographed dances. She continued to be a performer almost all of her long life, but she was also much more than that as a dancer, and later as a leader of her own group, and finally as a choreographer of the human condition through relating dance to mythological themes.

Doris Humphrey began as a dancer and ended up as a choreographer, but what is more important here, is that she became a choreographer of the human condition—the human condition as it could be if it were realizable in its more idealized form. It arose out of her love of dance, but as she grew her consciousness expanded and she found her life calling for more than she had earlier realized was possible. As she reached her middle years her horizon of the meaning of dance expanded with the expansion of her consciousness. Furthermore, in the process of its so doing she herself became a thoroughgoing humanist. Her life gives credence to the spirit of humanism. Her humanism centered around the relations of the individual to the group. Both of these women depicted the human condition, each in her own way.

Though it was very much through their own means that these two women determined to become Denishawn dancers, they had no great intentions in their beginnings, I believe, to determine their lives. Perhaps it is important to recall that it was not until 1920 that women gained the right to vote in the United States. In that year Martha Graham became twenty-six and Doris Humphrey twenty-five.

Women had little reason to believe that they could determine their own lives during those early years—though, of course there have been major exceptions. However, the path for Martha Graham was the easier one, for as she said in *Blood Memory:*

> my parents never objected to my becoming a dancer. They didn't say, *No, you won't become a dancer.* They never interrupted me. I could do anything I wanted. . . . I have always been myself in that sense.

But to become a Denishawn Dancer the path was difficult, indeed. Still she determined to become one, and she did.

The basic reason for the difficulty was that she was twenty-two and had never had training as a dancer. Out of her determination and hard work she became a lead dancer, and when she had a falling out with Ted Shawn, she set out on her own. When he insisted upon payment for any of the works that she had done as a Denishawn dancer, she had no choice, but to form her own company and to choreograph her own dances out of her own body. She was going on thirty-two, and though she had been forced to do so, she determined her own life then and from that time onward. And that self that she determined was one that bears the name of genius. And probably a woman had almost to be of that caliber to determine her self in those days. Self determinations were not the mode for a sex that had only been given voting rights a bare dozen years before.

Doris Humphrey had at least as difficult a time determining her own life. As a dance teacher she was largely the support of her parents. It was not until she found a substitute for herself as a teacher in her hometown that she felt free enough of familial obligations to be able join the Denishawn dancers. She was going on twenty-three when she began to determine a bit of her life—the dance portion. She began to choreograph successfully almost at once—solos at first and then group works. But the Denishawn schedule interfered with her choreography. It was not until she was free of the road traveling during the year 1926-27 that she was able to put into practice at all once again, some of the thoughts that she had been having about choreography. Her early choreography had been very successful, but the schedule the Densishawn troupe had to follow exhausted her and prevented her during that time from fulfilling her choreographic destiny. And then when the reorganized Denishawn insisted on allegiance to them in ways she could not countenance, she left—actually she was voted out—and formed her own company with Charles Weidman. That was how she came to determine her life. It was more than difficult at all times, but the lovely aesthetic of *Air on the G String* and the power and grandness of the conception of *New Dance* were testimony to her determination of a self of the kind that only genius can make. She showed how individuals, though remaining individuals can still foster the upward movement of the group. It was her philosophy fulfilled in the dance, and then her efforts, even when it was physically difficult for her to do so, fostering dancers and dance itself, she displayed that philosophy to the end of her life.

In both of these women the self determinations were, I feel, somewhat reluctant, at least compared to men at that time. I have the sense that the self determinations had to be, to some extent, forced from the outside in order to be initiated. Once initiated, however, they determined the remainder of their lives through hardships and the hardest imaginable physical work. The reluctance should be understandable considering how little women were able to determine about their lives in those days. My mother was thirty-two when women got the vote in the United States. She always voted, but she did so by asking my father for whom she should vote, and, then I gathered, so voted. When John F. Kennedy entered politics, however, she became more active, for she too was an Irish Catholic, Massachusetts voter. For her work he sent her a card on her seventy-fifth birhday. It took that strong emotional commitment to lead her to be more self determining politically. The reluctance of women to be self determining, compared with men, is, I think, with us still even in this era of Women's Liberation.

Self determinations should not have to be only the function of powerful loyalties or of genius, however. It should be the gift of all those blessed with consciousness, and that includes all undamaged human beings, for all have that prerogative. As I see it, each time we determine what we are to do in a problematical situation, and do it, the more the habit of determining ourselves becomes the result. It is the practice of self determinations that leads to more and more determinations. Women, I believe, are still generally somewhat handicapped in that regard, though circumstances are changing. But one of the southern states, still perhaps, or until recently anyway, ceded to the husband whatever money a woman brought with her into a marriage. No self determination can come from that practice. And the years of slavery—who can assess what they did to aspirations of self determination? Family determination was the most successful refuge, and it was often broken into at the whim of a white master. Neither of these outcomes provide for the practice of self determination. We have a long way still to go.

But we will not go anywhere in the direction of self determinations unless we know what they are, and that they grow as any other set of activities do, with practice and dedication.

CHAPTER X

Fostering Disinterested Interest

The *Boston Review* some time ago published a very valuable series of articles which contrasted "patriotism" with what their correspondent called "cosmopolitanism." One of those who responded to the issue questioned the possibility of anything beyond a kind of nationalist patriotism, for that is in part what the discusssion was about. Pannationalism was doubted by that responder, because the writer was assuming that human consciousness would have to be greater than it is if anything like cosmopolitanism were to occur. I believe the writer is, at least in part, correct, for the ordinary level of consciousness too often lacks the *disinterested interest* that would be required for some such view to be adopted. I say 'some such view' because I am not at all convinced that cosmopolitanism, as it had been set out there, is in our best interests, or that that would be the proper word for what would be the right concept. But if the writer were espousing the notion that because human nature has always been inadequate to the task of going beyond national patriotism, and more significantly, *always will be*, I would have to disagree. I would disagree, because I believe that consciousness can be developed well beyond what it has been in our past.

I have indicated that consciousness arises naturally during development, and I also believe that a reflective consciousness also arises simply out of our ordinary human experiences. But the quality of disinterested interest that arises out of that consciousness, and especially arises out of our reflective consciousnesses, is not simply given under our usual upbringings nor through our usual educations. Disinterested interest requires the development of attitudes fostered within consciousness that go beyond what we have hitherto expected from upbringing or education. In a sense then consciousness can be developed as it has never been done before, and disinterested interests, are as we know, already possible within our current knowledge. More thoughtfulness would be required, and more thought and care given to the development of both consciousness and to the intentional development of the attitude of disinterested interest than we have usually given to them, however. How to foster that development is known, though we have not often made use of that knowledge. The development of disinterested interest that goes hand in hand with the development of consciousness requires a fostering that is subtle and, I believe, new to most of us.

There has been no research focussed directly on the development of consciousness—nor disinterested interest, I should add. That is in part the case because researchers have not defined consciousness, and our reflective consciousnesses, as I have defined them here. Nor have they defined them in a fashion that would call for a development such as I think is possible, because their notions around an improved consciousness have had to do with an increase in concentration rather than in an *expansion* and integration of our experiencings of our awarenesses. And, of course, our ability to concentrate increases from childhood to adulthood, especially when what is concentrated upon is self determined. But I believe that the most important aspects of the developments of consciousness are overlooked in that view of consciousness. There are, however, research findings on the development of cognition which are relevant to how consciousness develops. Recall that some of the research has indicated that between the ages of about six to eight the average child is able to grasp that the amount of liquid remains constant no matter whether the container is wide and flat or thin and tall. Before that age children tend to pay attention only to the height—one factor—rather than to the height and width—two factors. Accordingly, pouring the liquid from a tall and narrow container into a short and wide container causes them to conclude that the amount of liquid has decreased. Though consciousness defined as the awareness of an awareness arises at some point probably on the average around three years of age, this set of awarenesses apart from the child's interests takes longer for the child to achieve. The added complexity arises from the fact that the awarenesses involve objects and a situation outside the child's usual egocentric interest. This ability to develop a removal from the self is an aspect of what can become disinterested interest at work in an early stage. It arises out of our naturally given, natural in terms of normal development, that is, ordinary human consciousness.

The ability to read, that is, to read in the sense of being able to look at the series of printed words and at the same time grasp the meaning expressed in a sentence or a paragraph, also is a function of consciousness. Reading requires that the child be aware of the printed words in sequence, and aware simultaneously of the overall meaning expressed that is not in any of the words. This is a complex integration that can only occur in consciousness. Reading can also be a factor in the development of disinterested interest, but only if the reading is both interesting and meaningful personally to the child. Traditionally, students were taught to read in the second grade—when the average student reached an age of seven years. That tradition has been lost in recent years because of an overemphasis on reading compared to a lessened emphasis on mathematics, and even less emphasis, especially, to any of the personal interests of the individual child. Is it any wonder that we turn out so few people literate in mathematics and science when so much emphasis is placed on reading over those other subjects? But it is the unusual child who before the age of seven, while looking at, seeing, and aware of the sequence of the printed words, can at the same time look through that sequence of printed words for the unseen meaning—that is also there for those who can read. When we recall that to be able really to read means grasping the meaning of phrases and sentences, and hopefully the sense of the whole story, it should be plain that real reading is not likely to be an accomplishment of the ordinary child before seven years. Consciousness, recall, requires that we be aware of two separated events—here the arbitrary spelling of those printed English words, and the meaning of the sentences that make up the story—*simultaneously*. That integration for the average child, just as is understanding that the amount of liquid stays the same no matter what its height, awaits development and requires that integrated set of awarenesses which define consciousness.

It is true that reading can foster disinterested interest, but that can only occur if the child is able to choose what book to read for his or her own purposes. A mere mouthing of worded-sounds while looking at a printed word must not be accepted as reading. It is only when the child looks at the series of printed words, but is able to grasp the unseen story being told through the sentences and paragraphs, that s/he can read. When that kind of reading is ingrained the child has arrived at what is not an entirely egocentric interest. Though the topic has to fit what the child in interested in, once engrossed in the reading the awarenesses of the child tend to be overwhelmingly involved in what engrosses him or her for its own sake. The child can be lifted out of himself by what he reads.

So being able to read for meaning is also a start upon the development of disinterested interest, because the child finds much in the written world to pique his or her interests, and expand them beyond the egocentric needs and interests to which we human beings are so prone. Of course we *begin* to learn out of our personal interests, but reading can take us out of those narrower interests, and lead us into the direction of interests in the world in its own terms, into disinterested interests. Reading does take us, real reading, that is, into the realm of another world, real or imaginary, and then we are taken out of ourselves and our little world into a much wider one.

How to begin this process of reading, involving as it does the singular ability of what is read to release the child from his natural egocentricity, cannot begin arbitrarily, if it is to serve the purpose of engaging the child in disinterested interests. This new way of beginning, I am sorry to report, has seldom been made use of in school settings. And furthermore since real reading requires that the average child be around seven years of age, the better way to begin is not only available earlier, but preferable to the traditional ones. The best way to begin is through all childrens' deep interests in expressing themselves. They do this with any means at their disposal. The ones that are most available in a school setting are speaking, drawing, and acting out their interests expressively. Speaking is, of course, a skill that all children have through which to express themselves by the time they enter school, but having all twenty-five to thirty or more students speak at once in school is impractical. Drawing can be done essentially silently, as can writing. But writing requires a developed skill that the average five year old has not yet achieved; drawing as expressivity requires no tuition—and all children have some ability to draw. Give a two year-old a crayon and she draws—or at least scribbles.

Furthermore, all three of these modes of expression—speaking, acting out, and drawing, and of course writing in time—arise out of the childrens' desires to express themselves. Reading, on the other hand, like listening to someone lecture, involves a giving over of one's own expressivity and personal interests to attend to another's ideas. That is a truly hard task to do for all of us—children or adults. It is strange that we ask precisely of children in school what most of us always find most difficult to do, but traditionally in schooling we do just that. I suggest that neither an expanded consciousness, nor disinterested interests can be developed out of didactic methods imposed on the child. I believe that that may be one reason why disinterested interests out of well developed consciousnesses are not more prevalent in our culture.

I believe that drawing is the most basic means of expression that the school has. We can start the process of education with, say five or even four year-olds easily in that way. They cannot be expected to write yet, and it is wrong to ask them to learn to read, for that is yet to be learned—hopefully by around age seven. And, more important, most children at four or five are not yet ready to put together print and meaning. Speech and their meaning, however, they already have developed as a highly routinized skill; drawing retains the childrens' expression of their own self interests just as speaking does. When they are encouraged to express their experiences in drawing several beneficial results occur. First, the children are expressing what matters to them, what pertains to them. Their interest is accordingly guaranteed. I have observed a five year-old child spend about twenty minutes sewing a cloth purse for his mother. No teacher expects to keep a child that young at an assigned task that long. But a self assigned task has expressivity, and what matters to the child, the child's feeling value, and interest to bolster it. Drawing can have that quality. Drawing also has the advantage of increasing the child's dexterity and skill in manipulating instruments. Several skills are thereby practiced at once: handling the implement, expressing what interests her, and developing the skill in drawing. What the child draws, furthermore, gives the teacher a clue as to how to gain that child's interest to carry on his or her education further.

Once the drawing has been completed the teacher can ask the child to tell what is happening in the drawing. As the child begins to speak the teacher can print below the drawing what the child is saying. In this way the child is able to begin to grasp that the drawing, the print and the child's own speech share some relation. This is especially important in those cases where little reading is done at home. Seeing the print formed under the drawing by the teacher the child begins to grasp that what comes out of his mouth in one rush of feeling has a counterpart in what is printed. Such vague senses of relations increase meaning, for meaning arises out of relations. In addition, learning to read is assisted, because the drawing overtly displays its meaning so that the child has both the drawing and the print to depend upon when she returns to see what she meant. The child begins to see what the printing-aided by the drawing means.

What is unrelated to us as children—or adults—remains meaningless. Our relatives, our relations, are meaningful. The child's drawing, speaking, and the teacher's printing can in this way begin to carry the same meaning for the child: They are all parts of one meaningful set of activities. If one watches and listens to a child draw, one sees and hears immediately that the drawing is accompanied by speaking sotto-voice as the child indicates what is happening. I recall a child drawing an animal on the edge of a pond, and as he drew he said aloud, "And he's sliding, sliding into the water," as he put the finishing touches on the drawing. When the teacher prints the story of the happening under the drawing, the child has a record of the remembered meaning and the printed meaning all in one unit. When the child is encouraged to copy the print, the way to writing begins. For the printed words remain related to the drawing, to the speaking, and to the child's own meaning. Furthermore, the print that tells the story is a symbolic way of representing the drawing, just as the drawing was a symbolic representation of the child's experience. The drawing serves to develop the symbolizing process that is basic to reading, that is also basic to the expansion of consciousness itself, and, potentially, to the development of more disinterested interests. And it is our ability to symbolize that is basic to knowing, to cognition, to the knowledge which education means to foster. And, of course, the drawing as a representation, a symbolic expression of the child's lived experience is lively and compelling, not a static doing just for the sake of doing. Increasing the symbolization of experience into cognitions is basic to all education.

Drawing is also better than having the child tell what she is interested in even though she may speak reasonably well. Children's memories are full of images rather than words—remember Einstein's expression of the imaged nature of his thinking process—and drawings can use these images quite directly. Teachers often ask students to report on something interesting that they did during the summer vacation. Drawings can replace that. The speaking, however, unless it is written down or printed by the teacher, which is seldom the case, is lost. Speaking is more ephemeral than a drawing is, for the drawing provides a permanent record. Besides, few children listen to what their classmates did when what he or she did personally is what is most fascinating always. Furthermore, since we are talking about a child in a classroom, the child may be inhibited about speaking publicly, as we all are, about what matters to us. On the other hand the drawing can be a relatively private expression of the self. However in classrooms where drawing is encouraged, there often is a hum of talking as each child expresses in speech as well as drawing what intrigues her or his interest. The drawing becomes an aid to increasingly skilled activities of hand and eye coordination; such skills become ever more important in this abstracted computer age. In time, the printing underneath the drawing by the teacher, which tells what the child has said, also becomes a record of the child's interests as they develop. These continual indicators of the child's developing interests can be used by the teacher in fostering the child's further education, that is, toward what the teacher knows the child must learn. But for the child the record becomes a means also for examining the work itself, and learning to read it. For like the rest of us, the child is interested in her own work and her own doings.

This examination of his own work is at one remove from the activity itself, and allows the child to take a more objective view of what was done earlier; the children can, and do in time, stand back from the work as they could not in the heat of its expression. This standing back allows the child to pay attention to aspects of the drawing, and of the printing that were not present during the activities themselves That can lead to intentions to improve the drawing, or it can lead to intentions to improve the printing, or it may lead to intentions to improve what has been said, or the way of saying it. Or, instead of improvements it can lead to new, but related thoughts that extend the child's interests. When the children are at a remove from the drawing they can assess it in a less fraught fashion. This remove lends itself to an increase in objectifying the work which is an aspect of what in time can become a disinterested interest.

Expanded interests and personal standards have an opportunity to develop out of the enterprise that has now taken on a more objective and extended meaning—the story is known, so it may quite easily be read and contemplated. What is now out there, though it originated from the child, allows the child to begin to move on the way to developing a habit that has a quality already of disinterested interests: the artistry of the drawing, or of the printing, or of what is said, or the way of saying it, new thoughts, or any or all of these can become the central focus. They may not so become, of course, but they may. Disinterested interests arise out of personal interests and personal standards for events that engage us, but are very different from the egocentric, self satisfaction of needs. The need for expression that was there originally, is no longer present during the later contemplation.

The pressing need becomes a thing of the past. The drawing, the printing, and its total meaning now lend themselves to contemplation rather than the satisfaction of needs, and contemplation is a necessary factor for the development of disinterested interests.

To get a sense of the importance of these procedures let us consider what is usually done in schooling. The child's interests are not paramount, but instead schooling and reading are what dominate most current primary education. The child, even at five or earlier, when most children are not capable of anything but a kind of memorization of the print seen, and of the sound made. is pressed to learn to read by some sort of arbitrary method. Some children, a minority, do learn to read, do actually learn to read so that someday they may read not word by word but even paragraph by paragraph—which is what we should be striving for as a standard of reading anyway. But the latter accomplishment is not a function of the methods of reading so far developed. The accomplishement is a function of a particular child's personal ability. The conventional methods of teaching reading, which are too often used for all children, and indiscriminately, do not honor the relations between speaking and expressing their meaning which all children have when they enter school. And then what often passes for reading is the child's ability to sound out what the print stands for in sound, one sound even, at a time. That then satisfies those who have not grasped that reading truly involves: Living in a world not present: Seeing simultaneously the print and the meanings, actually, seeing through the visible print and into the invisible story unfolding in the *imagination* of the child. For reading is tied really to the child's ability to imagine a scene that does not appear anywhere in the printed story.

The invisible story unfolding before the child via the visible print is what true reading involves. Too often reading is assumed to have occurred when the bare sounding out of the name or word is given. Meaning is often considered to be irrelevant in assessments of this sort. Indeed, in many reading programs meaning is not mentioned and not even acknowledged as relevant—and in some cases as even existent at all. Of course, because human beings are inherently relational, and accordingly grasp meanings everywhere, the child will assign meanings to things, because it is our very natures to do so. Meaning arises out of relations. What is unrelated to us is meaningless. But our relations, our mothers and fathers and sisters and brothers are meaningful to us. Under many systems of teaching reading, however, meaning, our formation of relations of one thing with another, is largely ignored. Meaning, however, the individual child's meaning that the child wants to express, is central when reading begins as drawing and printing—which the child then reads out of her own deep interests exactly what matters to her.

It is out of this latter kind of reading that disinterested interests are aided in arising. Most of us educated persons achieve that level of reading somehow, but on our own. For no one actually knows how it is that a human being becomes a reader, a reader of stories at first, and perhaps later a reader of paragraphs dealing with complex social or philosophical thoughts. Reading meanings to oneself is the aim, not reading aloud word by word. Indeed, reading aloud is a skill in itself, but it differs markedly from the skill of reading thoughts laid out on the printed page. Reading thoughts is seldom taught, but it is learned anyway by readers all over the world and in whatever direction the print moves. However, it is out of our interests of honing any of our own skills that disinterested interest arises. That is why I feel that the artistic discoveries in the caves of France are so important: The skillfulness of the drawings and paintings indicate the bourgeoning of disinterested interest early on in our human existences. But we have never set out intentionally to foster that frame of mind.

We foster learning what the culture already has set forth as worth knowing. We attempt to instill high standards of achievement in our educational systems. But achievement is not learning—learning arises out of the fascination with the topic rather than to achieve a prize. So we set up norms and expectations in the various school subjects, and expect that the children pass tests that indicate that they have achieved this or that level of learning at the same time for all. Those that are quick and find such learning easy, do well; those that do not, do poorly, and may even be assessed as failing. In none of this great emphasis on achievement is there the means for learning and developing disinterested interests. The child's total interest under such conditions has to be in achieving the highest grade according to the goals set forth by the school. That interest in achievement removes the child from honing his or her skills, and is, therefore, deleterious to the development of disinterested interests. Disinterested interest involves at first achievements directly related to the child's interest. Gradually, the child's interests become caught by the activities themselves, and the way to disinterested interests has begun. Achievement of standards set by the school for all children takes the child away from his or her own standards to those outside of the child. The engagement with the achievement of externally set standards really precludes the development of skill and artistry—except by chance and for some unusual individuals.

Achievement as the final aim fosters only self-interested interests. Competition leading to achievement, however, is what has been happening in the schools in our culture. We thereby foster external achievements over the internal ones that lead to disinterested interests.

Some persons, perhaps most, do achieve the state, more or less, of disinterested interest anyway. But the highest and most meaningful standards are those that arise from the individual himself. I know better than anyone else what I am trying to compose. And I know whether I have reached that standard or failed to reach it. And when I have been praised for work *I* did not prize, I not only did not accept that evaluation, but I lost respect for those who gave it. It was extraneous to my evaluation of the work, and worthless to me and my personal internal standards. It is those personal and individual standards that go along with disinterested interest, for those standards apply only to me and not to any other. That attitude toward my own work helps to give me the freedom to assess the works of others with disinterested interest, just as it also aids me in developing my own.

We have a long way to go in developing the ubiquitousness of disinterested interests in humanity, but we actually do know the way to achieve it, and, most important, we do know what disinterested interest is. Disinterested interest is the ability to pay attention to outside events in their own terms. It means that we do not impose our wishes and desires, or our standards upon them, but allow the events to occur in their own ways. We may then evaluate an event negatively or positively, but we have first allowed whatever it was to exist in its own terms. Fostering disinterested interest may not be a cure all, but it could go a long way toward remedying some of the problems that our failure to employ it have been fostering.

Disinterested interest is a quality in human beings that is supremely important. It takes us all the way back, or is it forward, to what is truly human in humanity. Disinterested interests are an essential ingredient of spiritual humanism. '

CONCLUSIONS

The human spirit does not necessarlily predispose us in the direction of a belief in, for example, a Great Spirit that might have been in existence when the Big Bang occurred. By my definition of the human spirit that conclusion would be a personal one. I have concluded on the basis of the assumptions I have articulated that I, at least, do not know. But I also do not know that the physicists and astronomers have it right either. I have to pass on that whole issue. But I think the atheists have to have it wrong. It seems to me that I have merely taken Nicholas of Cusa's assumptions to their logical conclusion. (And I am not at all sure that that is a good thing.) As a cardinal in the Roman Catholic Church, he concluded that in Christ, assumed to be both man and God, could be found the clue to the Deity. I am not a cardinal and am not making that assumption, but I would not be surprised if many would follow Cusa rather than me.

I do have strong caveats against a too easy a belief in the current *theory* of evolution—and it is a *belief* not a fact. That is why I am uneasy about it. Science may tell us *how* we got here; science cannot tell us *why* we are here. The latter is in the realm of belief and faith. But the theory of evolution does not at all tell us—we who register, who are aware of things and events, and who may even have a consciousness of something spiritual within us—it does not even tell us how we, as acknowledged bearers of all of these qualities, got here with those qualities. Certainly, the theory of evolution cannot tell us why we are here. Though I believe that some evolutionists may think that it can. It cannot.

At the crucial point of a needed explanation for the spirit which pervades humanity, the theory of evolution resorts to an unpredicted and unpredictable mutation. I require a theory that accounts for the totality of what is present in us human beings, not a theory that only accounts for a truncated portion of a whole human being. I think that we should all insist upon such a theory no matter what current doctrine suggests. And for me that theory must do so without recourse to the unpredictable, non scientific mutations upon which it is currently dependent.

Anthropomorphic optics, however, can become the primary human science, for consciousness falls within its enterprise and expertise as arising out of psychological processes. Physical theory is too far from the central issues of human conduct to be able, as Roger Penrose had hoped, ever to arrive at an understanding of the consciousness that allows us to live lives based upon our individual value systems. Only a psychology beginning in human perceptual awarenesses, thus an anthropomorphic optics, can extend human experiencings into the realm of human consciousness and human values and valuing to account for human conduct. So far, however, no theory of that psychological order has been mathematized to make it a complete science that would make it comparable to physical theories. I sometimes think that such a humanistic theory cannot be mathematized. I certainly no longer believe that mine can be mathematized, or, at least, that *I* could or would want to do so. Though I once did. Whether accepting the priority of the psychological will have a beneficial effect on theorizing in physics is too far beyond my competence to judge. But I think it would be nearsighted of them to reject that possibility out of hand. I invite them to engage in what is really the total scientific enterprise: to examine and reexamine the nature of their basic assumptions. I also invite the proponents of artificial intelligence to engage in the enterprise of examining precisely what intelligence in humanity consists of instead of assuming some common sense idea that by its very nature, not even ever having been investigated, has to be *pre*scientific.

But intelligence as an issue is, I believe, largely passe, anyway. I believe that we may now have left behind the Age of Intelligence, and may have finally entered the Age of Consciousness! And there can be no turning back. Consciousness has helped to establish and enlarge the role of feeling values in human conduct. The central place of our feeling values in the thinking that we have to engage in in living our lives makes quite plain the narrowness of AI as an enterprise. Just as the computers lack a thalamo-cortical-limbic system, so too do they overlook the power of human feelings as the basis for any really important motivation for thinking—whether it be theoretical thinking or thinking about the issues of one's daily life. And then the marriage of abstract mathematical thought to the instrumenatlly based measures of physics has its own effects. Not the least of these has been the abolition of any quality that could be called "spirit" from their instrumentally based physical measures by their initial assumptions and methods.

The Age of Consciousness, one could almost say, was largely initiated by William Shakespeare in his play, *Hamlet*. There, however, writing at the threshold of the Age of Consciousness, he displayed mainly the viscisitudes that can befall a human being newly beset with consciousness. It has taken longer for the slowness of humanity to grasp the positive side of consciousness. We have spent millenia now in using consciousness as an intelligence *weapon*. Only Socrates among all of the ancients clearly tried to use consciousness to consider human values—at least to some extent. The Romans were content to use consciousness to aid their intelligence in conquering the world—except perhaps for Marcus Aurelius. Their efficiency as soldiers, as planners, as organizers, yes, and even as executioners, was a function of the great *intelligence* they brought to bear on those enterprises. But they did not carry forth their consciousness into other directions. It was the Judeo-Christian tradition that came closest to going beyond using consciousness for purposes of intelligence by focussing upon the individual's conscience. But the Judeo-Christian values revolved around their religion based moral values rather than humanly based ethical ones.

The Judeo-Christian moral stance, I believe, has submerged whatever ethical possibilities there could be for humanity under its moral stance. Morality's purview is too limited in this complex Age of Consciousness—but I cannot go into that here. It takes in only the single and direct relationship between the believer and his religion's values. Morality does not deal with the complications that every culture has to face whenever its denizens are not homogeneous. And the future appears to be one where homgeneity is less and less possible, or desirable, in a global world environment. The old Yugoslavian battle ground is, or should be, an anachronism in the modern world—though it is not. Heterogeneity is bound to be the case in the future. Our children know this. Today's world is one where our communications daily break down the boundaries that were once physical and everywhere. An ethical standard is what we now need.

And an aesthetic attitude is needed because of its central nature in helping to form *disinterested*, but at the same time a wholly *interested* living atttitude. It is that attitude that I believe may be central to an ethical over a moral view, and it is that attitude that can begin to wean us from the prejudices which are so common to ever error-prone humanity. We are still in the early phase of the Age of Consciousness. Our awareness that we have arrived there will be a great aid to speeding the process so that the whole of humanity may participate in it. A spiritual humanism is, I believe, the means for the implementation of that attitude, and its hope for the future.

Finally, it is consciousness that gives us some ability to determine how we will conduct ourselves in the world. Developing a set of values by which to live is not an idle wish, but a real possibility now for persons with consciousness. It is true, however, that feeling values are not simply given to us as awareness is, and consciousness also is. For that consciousness which arises during early childhood develops more and more complexly over time. In the early phases, at least, consciousness seems to follow its own schedule without effort on our part. But we do have to work on the development of values even with consciousness, I believe, though some persons appear to come to valuing concerns naturally. I know that a concern with valuing was not at all natural to me who always was a thinking person in Carl Jung's terms. I believe that he was at least partly right in suggesting that thinking and feeling, and therefor thinking and valuing are opposed. We cannot be concerned centrally with the values of what arises in our lives, if as Einstein or I did, one believes that devising a general theory was the most important value in life. Devising a psychological theory was how I spent my life. What I have written here is an attempt to bring that thinking I always prized so highly to fruition in a value area. And one of the most important values we can have, I believe, is to foster disinterested interests in all of us.

But what of Cusa's thesis in our so-called postmodern times? What happens to our spirit when we finally become brain dead? It has been our modern conclusion most often that that spirit dies with the brain. But when we consider registration there is no end to it even in the dust that we all do become. Our physical-physiological beings have thus become one with the earth. And our spiritual being, what of it? One answer is, it is gone, departed with the brain and body. That has been the modern answer. But it could also be that the spirit has joined the larger Spirit—whatever Its quality may be. We cannot know.